Ursula-

Keep inspiring!

[signature]

P.S. The future is female :)

ZONED IN™

The Mental Toughness Required for a World-Class YOU

Sheryl Kline M.A. CHPC

For dad,

Thank you for instilling in me
what I hope to instill in all those who read this book.

"I believe in you always,
and you can achieve whatever you put your mind to."

CONTENTS

INTRODUCTION

There are similarities and differences between world-class performers and everyone else. Generally, we all have a similar range of emotions, from positive and encouraging to negative and defeating. But there's one factor that separates the best from the rest: world-class performers know how to use their thoughts and emotions to their advantage on the march from good to great. They know how to be mentally tough.

The following chapters include curated research, inspirational stories, and personal examples to make the most important point in this book: *you can* learn how to be mentally tough, plan for what you yearn for, and make consistent progress towards your own personal Olympics.

Before we begin, it's imperative to reflect. Have your thoughts and emotions ever held you back from something you wanted and deserved? Have you ever prepared relentlessly, been 100% capable, then showed up and *not* delivered? Do any past failures or future fears keep you from achieving something important to you? These fears and failures are all very under-standable, valid, and real, but they can disable your ability to be your best. Maybe you have a partner, children, aging parents, or a career that requires you to be very agile. Whatever your circumstances, you are a multi-sport athlete who has a champion within. But without the proper tools, it's possible to limit yourself—by what you think is possible, by your current circumstances, by your past experiences, or by your future worries.

I certainly did. Whether in school, playing sports, or well into my career, I made sure I prepared, and I knew I was capable. Yet when it came time to compete, all the hard work seemed to be for naught. I showed up, but I couldn't deliver, especially when it mattered most. My thoughts and emotions affected my concentration, motivation, and ability to reach my potential. Because I didn't have the tools to manage my thoughts and emotions, they disabled my progress and performance.

I put limitations on myself based on how I grew up and the perceptions I had about myself. As a young person, I was surrounded by uber-achievers in an ultra-small and competitive private high school. That set the stage for me early on—feeling like I wasn't good enough to be like 'them'. 'They' always got A's. 'They' took AP classes. 'They' were going to an Ivy, Berkeley, UCLA, and so on. It was incredibly frustrating because I was told I was just as capable as 'them', and I certainly worked just as hard.

I was fortunate to have encouragement and support from teachers, coaches, and most importantly my father telling me to "Be resilient and focus; you can do whatever you put your mind to." That sounded like excellent advice, but at the time, I didn't know how to recover from failure or perform under pressure. Even though I was capable and gritty, I kept falling short when I knew I had the potential to achieve more.

I wondered how Olympians could practice for years (in many cases decades), suffer defeats and injuries, and deal with people saying they can't do it, yet keep on going. They dust themselves off, get back into the arena, and give their best performance in the most important moments. They're like warriors who deny defeat when everyone else retreats. So, I decided to find out how world-class athletes could train their entire life, then show up under intense pressure and deliver in those crucial moments—consistently.

Since then, I've spent the better part of three decades studying applied sport psychology, working with world-class athletes and business people to crack the code and master the mental toughness needed for achieving your best. I've dedicated my life's work to helping others take control of accomplishing what they want and deserve. The framework I created has helped high-level athletes and business professionals to realize a transformation that they had inside but were unable to access.

What I've discovered and what I believe to my core is that *we are all capable of more*. Please don't misunderstand me. We do *a lot,* and whether you're spearheading initiatives, at the pinnacle of your career, or experiencing utter confusion and stagnation, I honor you for what you *have* done up to this point.

Now, by virtue of consuming this content, you are committed to learning, growing, and improving, which is world-class in and of itself. So please stand up and take a bow. Really. (If you have worked with me personally or have been to any of my global workshops, you should be very familiar with this request!) The compound effect of successes—large and small—is vital to our grand success. We must recognize our successes and be proud of them on our march to any new level of ambition.

Often, it's easy to lose sight of the lives we've touched, the progress we've made, and what we've given to others. This affects our momentum, motivation, and confidence. Take a moment to have gratitude for yourself, and for the good you have already put into the world. Then you'll be ready to move forward.

How Do We Become Our Best Selves?

How do we gain the clarity and resilience to persevere when our journey gets hard? It always seems to get hard, doesn't it? Moreover, if we prepare relentlessly, so we are capable of winning a gold medal, how do we arrive optimally in those important moments? How can we summon the champion within to make all the striving, sacrificing, and effort worth it?

There are legendary scientists and human performance experts such as Anders Ericsson (*Peak*), Carol Dweck (*Mindset*), Angela Duckworth (*GRIT*), and Brendon Burchard (*High Performance Habits*), just to name a few, who have spent their lives proving that if we think, plan, and work in a certain way, we can achieve way beyond the standard norm. They have proven that our mindset and habits are more important than what we are innately born with. They have also provided us with the proof and materials to achieve our dreams. But what is the foundation where these epic materials sit: quicksand or solid ground? How can we lean on this science and build world-class mental toughness, so we can transform from ordinary to our next level of extraordinary?

Mental toughness provides the foundation required to dream, plan, and achieve our best. Without it, we are vulnerable to what others say, our past failures, our worries about possible future failures, and our doubts. Plus a whole host of other thoughts and emotions that we relinquish power to and that can disable our chances of achieving what we want and deserve.

You see, work ethic is incredibly important, but unfortunately it's not enough. I'm sure you work incredibly hard and your ambitions are high, or you wouldn't be taking the time to learn and grow. But to achieve something new or get to the next level, you must be mentally tough too, and this is something you *can* learn. The tools to accomplish this are not gifts reserved for the elite few. They are learned skills that you will access in this book.

I've been blessed to share my ZONED IN Mental Toughness framework at Google Ventures, Autodesk, Bank of America, VMware, and many other companies in San Francisco, Silicon Valley, and worldwide as well as coaching and training people from all over the world. The feedback has been absolutely amazing, and it's my honor to share it with you.

It is my sincere hope that the coming chapters will unlock what is already yours, encourage you to dream even bigger than you currently do, and give you the character to keep going when others do not.

About This Book

This book is for those ready to 'go pro' in their commitment to mastering the thoughts and emotions necessary to champion their results. It's for those discovering a new ambition and those taking their current ambition to the next level—in their relationships, on the sports field, or in their career. It's for those ready to learn a new set of mental toughness tools to achieve a greater sense of contribution and joy. It's for those who are willing to put in the work and believe in the possibilities of what lies ahead for them.

This book will help you become ZONED IN so you can:

- Get crystal clear on what you want, discover why you care so deeply, and design a custom plan to help you get there.

- Understand how to manage your thoughts and emotions in high-pressure situations.

- Know how to be accountable for your success.

- Understand how to set effective objectives and make steady progress.

- Discover how to manage your internal voice and be able to Think2Win.

- Become more proficient even when you are unable to physically practice.

- … and much more!

Moving forward, you will be taken on a journey of planning and progress, but it requires that you accept the challenge to learn and then commit to putting in the effort. Your world will be open to the same content, tools, and challenges as world-class athletes and business professionals, who are in many cases no different than you.

This book will be interactive to have the most impact. Each chapter of ZONED IN will explain one module of my framework and guide you through the ZONED IN Acceleration

Exercises, so you can apply what you learn and create a master plan for yourself.

It's Time!

I believe that we all have a gift placed inside us, with a limited amount of time to bring it into the world. I wholeheartedly believe that it's time. It's time for us to show up in this world as we are meant to. It's time to take what matters most to the next level. It's time to understand that we have greatness within us already.

Let's believe that the world is conspiring to coax this gift out of us, and the world desperately needs to see it now. It's time for us to inspire others to do the same by leading as an example. Whether you consider yourself a role model or not, *you are*. People are watching, following your lead, and it's usually the ones you care about the most.

It's time to understand that the only limitations are those we put on ourselves, and the only dream that is impossible is the one we cannot see. We all have room for improvement—whether it's in our work, our relationships, or our personal wellness. What is most important to you right now? How can this time around be different or even better if you learn how to be mentally tough? Let's lay a solid foundation together, so you can have the mental toughness to make consistent progress towards your finish line.

Here's the amazing thing. You are not going at it alone. Beyond the pages of this book are resources to champion your efforts and a community waiting to cheer you on, challenge you, and help you. When you get to the end of this book, I will be waiting at the finish line, cheering and taking your hand to keep going. You just need to commit and believe that—yes—it is your time. We will rise, together.

Are you in?

"ZONED IN™"
Mental Toughness
Framework

Chapter 1

GET TO KNOW YOURSELF

"Every man, when he gets quiet, when he becomes desperately honest with himself, is capable of uttering profound truths. We all derive from the same source. There is no mystery about the origin of things. We are all part of creation, all things, all poets, all musicians; we have only to open up, to discover what is already there." – Henry Miller

Clarity is not static. It can be a fickle friend, but one we must actively pursue on our quest to be our best. World-class performers are remarkably clear about what their heart is telling them to strive for and why they care so deeply about it. We must be clear too, but it's also important to accept that our obligations change, as do our interests and personal missions. That's not just okay—it can be exciting and scary too. Before we can gain the mental toughness to be our best, it's vital to be very clear about what we yearn for. We must take inventory of who we are now, where our priorities lie, and which ambitions matter most to us right now.

At the Ambition Checkpoint

I had a conversation with one of my oldest and dearest friends a couple years ago that struck me as odd at first. She asked, "Do you ever feel like a plastic bag, drifting through the wind, wanting to start again …?" I recognized the opening lyrics to Katy Perry's song *Firework*. My friend seemed off. Not her usually present, fun, happy, and courageous self. It was strange, because she's so accomplished. She had raised happy, productive, and conscientious kids. She worked doing what she loved. She had a few half-marathons under her belt, a loving family, and a great group of friends. After many conversations with her, I finally understood. She was at an *ambition checkpoint*.

Her kids needed her less, and she felt like there was more of her to give to her career. More people to serve and a legacy to create. It was inaction that made her feel she was off-purpose, like a plastic bag drifting through the wind. She was being blown around by her days, by her old routine, by other people's wants and needs, and by being 'busy' without being purposeful. Without defining her next level of ambition, she didn't have a plan to make progress. She knew there was more. More of a sense of contribution. More of a feeling of purpose. More joy. However, it wasn't until she decided to be satisfied where she *was* that she could open her eyes and commit to the possibilities of what *could be*.

Have you ever felt like there's more? When each day isn't met with the excitement, joy, and vibrancy that's possible? When you have that uncomfortable feeling—nothing horrible, just a feeling of your current circumstances not being quite right? Most of us have been there, in that 'not quite right' place. That place where we feel our best self is not showing up consistently, or at all. Our own ambition checkpoint.

See, we have a human drive to feel like we are living as our best selves.[1] When we aren't, we might get the tap on the shoulder to pay attention and next-level our efforts. When we're not making progress towards living into the best version of ourselves, it can mean we're not as happy as we could be.[2]

Maybe you're crushing it at work, but your relationships need extra attention. Maybe you're giving 100% to your family, but you've put aside your dreams and aspirations to serve others. Or possibly each of these 'buckets' is half-full and you're feeling bored and unchallenged.

If this sounds familiar, if you're at the checkpoint, it's time to raise awareness about your changing ambitions now. We must accept our past as the best we could have done at the time, and we must be satisfied with it to move on. We can ignore the tap on the shoulder that signifies a checkpoint, but it rarely retreats. And there's usually a price to pay if we neglect it for too long.

There is no more time to procrastinate. Yesterday has happened. It's history. What will you do going forward to be your best self? It's time to reassess your ambitions and think about who you want to become. Then you'll be able to see that person and become that person.

Are you ready to commit to yourself?

 ## ZONED IN Acceleration Exercise:

If you answered yes, please sign here:

I, _____, am committed to achieving more of what matters most to me. I acknowledge and I am satisfied with my past efforts. By signing here, I am committing to learning how to become mentally tough, so I can use my thoughts and emotions for consistent progress, and so I can have the impact that I know I am meant to have.

_____

_____

_____

_____

Taking Your Ambitions to the Next Level

When you've decided to move on from the checkpoint, it's time to take your ambition to the next level. If you've already climbed the ranks in a job you love, I hope you've celebrated that success wholeheartedly! But could you do even better? What would it be like to treat your team a little better, inspire them a little more, listen to their ideas more, or ask how they are doing more often? How could you take your performance to the next level and inspire your team to do the same? How could you create a more productive and sustainable workday?

Maybe you're re-entering the workforce, considering working again after raising a family, or ready for a change at work. You have a feeling that it's time to pivot, a voice telling you that there's more. If it's your **career** that requires your attention, it's time to listen. Whether your résumé and LinkedIn profile are brimming with current experience and accolades or not, it's time to confront the excuses head on. Look them in the eye and explain that although they are valid concerns, they will no longer hold you back.

If your next big challenge—the one you know deep down is asking you to pay attention—is your **relationships** or a specific relationship, it's time to take action. Sometimes, striving for the best relationships possible is the most honorable, challenging, and rewarding ambition begging for your attention right now.

Finally, we must examine how we are taking care of ourselves when it comes to exercise, nutrition, and relaxing/recharging. Maybe it's time to get into the best shape of your life. If you've had a health scare, what more do you need to take action? If not, don't wait for one!

What part of your personal **wellness** routine will you take to the next level, and who besides yourself will benefit? What will the outcome be if you don't start moving around more, meditating more, eating more fruits and vegetables and less processed food, forgiving yourself more, being happy more, and so on…?

Regardless of which ambition is most important to you right now—career, relationships, or personal wellness—you must decide whether you are going to be a quitter, a novice, a player, or a pro. Which part of your life are you going to take seriously and commit to improving? It's time to commit to the next level.

Keep in mind that quitting isn't always as awful as it sounds *if* you're quitting something that isn't serving you. The type of quitting I'm referring to here is giving up on something that you desperately want and deserve to have.

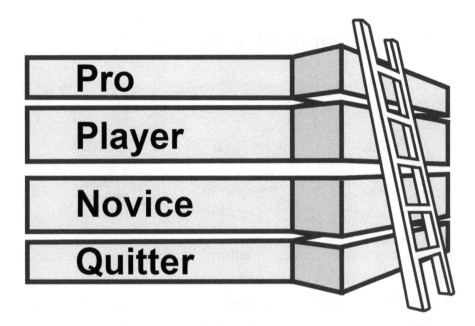

ZONED IN Acceleration Exercise:

Which level will you commit to now? And why is it important for you to do so?

_____

_____

_____

_____

_____

Which Bucket Do You Need to Fill?

Whether it's your career, relationship, or personal wellness 'bucket', they are all important and need consistent attention. I've seen from personal experience, three plus decades of research, and many clients that each bucket is no less important than the other. In other words, when one bucket is not attended to, the others suffer.

However, one bucket typically emerges as the most important at certain points in our lives. If we can focus on the most important bucket while tending to the others, this is a sustainable and holistic approach to becoming the best version of ourselves.

To become your best self, decide which of your buckets is the most important for you to fill right now. Which one is begging for your attention? Is it your career, your relationships, or your personal wellness that asks for your attention when the world slows down for a moment?

The longer we ignore the requests (the uncomfortable feeling that it's time to next-level an area in our life), the louder these requests become. Eventually, they will demand our attention, but it may be too late. We might quit our journey to advance in our job, give up on the dream of doing something we love, or settle for something (or someone) that we know is not quite right. We may have relationships that are not solidified or not repaired, then lose the ability to make them right.

Personal wellness bucket

Often, it's our personal wellness bucket that is the least forgiving. Maybe we have good intentions to make time for exercise, rest, and proper nutrition, but we fail to make it a consistent habit. We may get sick more often and become unable to achieve what we want and deserve. The requests on our personal wellness are subtle at first: a few extra pounds, persistent tiredness, aches and pains, or being in a fog. Then the requests turn into demands that we have no choice but to pay attention to.

Do you find it challenging to get into that exercise routine, eat better, or meditate? You are definitely not alone, but Dr. Steven Aldana, professor and CEO of Wellsteps says, "Unhealthy lifestyle behaviors are responsible for most chronic diseases. These diseases cause approximately 70 percent of all deaths and up to 75% of all healthcare costs. Lack of physical activity, poor diets and tobacco use are directly responsible for 70-90% of chronic diseases.[4]"

These statistics really hit home for me. I take my wellness as a personal obligation to myself and my family. Although I exercise regularly, I recently added meditation and mindfulness practice to my morning. What about you? How do these statistics make you feel, and what is one thing you can do next-level your personal wellness?

Career bucket

Have you ever felt like your current career isn't quite right? If it is right, maybe you haven't achieved the level of success you want and deserve? Or perhaps you're not getting recognized for your efforts? I've experienced all of these, and none of them are enjoyable.

More and more people I speak to have joy and challenge at the same time. They say things like: "I know what I want and what I should be doing, but I'm not taking the necessary consistent steps to get there." Having clarity is a joy and a relief, but sometimes it's scary too. Are you in this place? If so, it may be time to examine what you fear. Once you make peace with fear and learn how it can work with you instead of against you—that's when the magic happens. You'll learn how later in this book.

Feeling challenged, fulfilled, and recognized at work is important to your productivity, creativity, and joy. If this is an area you think about a lot right now, it might be time to take action for your next level of ambition here. Keep in mind, while you are the primary focus, there is a ripple effect on your colleagues, friends, and family when you achieve what is rightfully yours, which we'll look at in the next section.

Relationship bucket

Maybe your personal wellness and career buckets are doing well for now, which is amazing and so important. But what about your relationships? According to Chris Bailey, who wrote the book *The Productivity Project,* we aren't being as productive as we could be.

Whether it's work relationships, friends outside of work, or family, Bailey says, "People are why we do what we do, and why we push ourselves to accomplish more." If you've ever tried to make progress on a passion project (or any other project) when one or more of your inner circle relationships aren't in order, you'll have experienced this very point.

Lack of world-class relationships is no joke when it comes to our best work and overall joy. Is it even possible to be a sustainable high performer when our relationships are lacking? From my perspective, the research I have studied, and those who I have spoken to, absolutely not. So it's really important to pay attention to this bucket when you're climbing.

When we stop making progress on filling our most important bucket, it's like a slow leak in a balloon, draining us of our joy—and what we can give others. If this is you, how does it feel, and how does it affect you and those who matter most to you?

ZONED IN Acceleration Exercise:

Which bucket requires your attention and needs you to next-level your efforts right now? Is it your career, your relationships, or your personal wellness? Please explain why.

_____

_____

_____

_____

_____

Signs, then demands

You might think that these are things you can put off until another time, but when a bucket becomes close to empty, it may be too late. We get signs from whichever bucket needs our attention, and then we get demands.

This is an extreme example, but it proves my point. In March 2016, I had the flu. Rather than rest, I pushed through, taking care of business, and taking care of everyone else (but myself). Sound familiar? One morning, I was supposed to take my middle son Ryan to the airport. I knew I should stay in bed, but I got up anyway. When I went to brush my hair, my brush felt like a 10-pound weight. I eventually had to put it down, exhausted.

I am no Olympian, but I do exercise vigorously six days a week, so not being able to hold up a brush was a little concerning! I rested my forearms on my bathroom sink because they were so tired from seemingly nothing. The next thing I knew, I was staring at the ceiling of my bathroom. After a few stitches, a couple liters of fluid, an MRI, and an order to rest, I was on the mend.

My business was doing well. I was very intentional about strengthening my relationships with family, friends, and colleagues, and I was exercising and eating right. But I wasn't resting or recharging enough. I ignored the gentle requests, so my body eventually got frustrated with my stubbornness and demanded I next-level the way I recharge and take care of myself.

The effect on others

In all sincerity and certainly not to be disingenuous, taking care of ourselves isn't just about us personally. My mother passed away 19 years ago, when she was 69 years old. My oldest son Dan was just shy of 4 years old, Ryan was 1 and a half, and my daughter Megan wasn't even born yet. My mother was 40 pounds overweight, sedentary, had no social network to speak of, and was unhappy (a condition that has a cure). My mother suffered for a long time, and now my kids and I continue to suffer from missing her presence, her gentle words, and unconditional love.

When one of our buckets is running low, it's certainly not great for us, but who else suffers with us? How does this situation affect those who matter most to us: our colleagues, our friends, our partner, our children, anyone we are a role model for, or who we influence? *If we do not take care of our health, dedicate time to our relationships, or feel satisfied in our career, who suffers around us?*

Based on the number of local and global workshop attendees that have confided in me over the last two years, I would say there is an epidemic of extremely ambitious and hard-working professionals (especially women) who feel mediocre. While lack of recognition is the main culprit for this feeling at work, it stings even more at home. People are experiencing a lack of time with family, relationships that are becoming more distant and less fun, fewer close friends, and less time to spend with them. *What effect is your lack of time having on your loved ones?*

It is not just at home where feeling mediocre and not looking after our personal wellness is having an effect. In the workplace, Gallup puts a hefty price tag on U.S. employees not being their most engaged and productive selves as upwards of 550 billion dollars in corporate output[3]. What is the cost for your company or your career? Clearly, our wellness and happiness is no joke for us personally, as well as for our companies and for those we care about.

Lost revenue in part because people are not happy or fully engaged at work

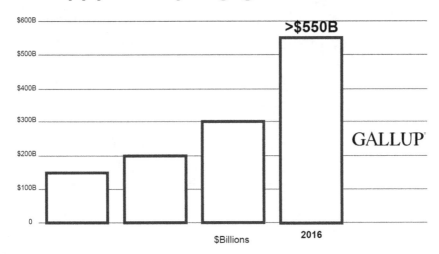

Consider the words of Ralph Waldo Emerson: *"The purpose of life is not to be happy. It is to be useful, to be honorable, to be compassionate, to have it make some difference that you have lived and lived well."* In other words, it's not just about us.

Maybe you consider yourself a role model or highly influential, or maybe you don't. Either way, you are, and you have the ability to create a compound effect of this power that already exists in you. When your personal wellness, career, and relationships buckets are full, they will have a ripple effect on those around you.

ZONED IN Acceleration Exercise:

Who else besides yourself will benefit if you commit and make progress towards what's most important to you now?

_____

_____

_____

_____

_____

Why Don't People Achieve Their Dreams?

There are many reasons why some people dream about wanting more, but don't go after it consistently. Here are a few persistent roadblocks when it comes to our success:

- **Doubt:** Am I good enough? Am I worthy of achieving more? Am I capable enough? Am I smart enough?

- **Fear:** What if I fail? What if it's too hard? What if I must sacrifice something else to achieve what's important to me?

- **Outside influences:** When others question my ambitions, what if they are right? When others who "have my best interest at heart" advise me to quit, should I take their advice?

Is it possible that you need to give yourself a little more compassion and perspective? If you doubt that those who have achieved great levels of success struggle too, just look at these two famous examples.[4]

J.K. Rowling had just gotten a divorce, was on government aid, and could barely afford to feed her baby in 1994, just three years before the first Harry Potter book, *Harry Potter and The Philosopher's Stone*, was published. She was so poor at the time that she couldn't afford a computer or the cost of photocopying the 90,000-word novel, so she manually typed out each version to send to publishers. It was *rejected dozens of times* until finally, a small London publisher named Bloomsbury gave it a second chance after the CEO's eight-year-old daughter fell in love with it. Did J.K. Rowling have fears or doubts after her manuscript was rejected so many times, especially when she had next-to-no financial resources?

Before Emily Blunt was a famous actress getting nominated for Golden Globes and landing leading roles, she could barely hold a conversation with her classmates. Between the ages of 7 and 14, she had a major stutter.

However, that all changed when one of Emily's school teachers encouraged her to try out for the school play—a totally unappealing idea given that she had such a hard time com-municating. Despite that, the teacher kept gently pressing, suggesting she try accents and character voices to help get the words out—and it worked. By the end of her teens, she had overcome her stutter and went on to have a very successful acting career.

Don't be tempted to think "That is them and this me." You can learn the very same world-class mindset that helped J.K. Rowling and Emily Blunt keep going. The same mental toughness tools that helped others who have achieved well beyond the standard norm.

Whether you're a famous author or writing your first book, a movie star or taking your first acting class, a world-class ath-lete or just beginning an exercise routine, a C-level executive or re-entering the workforce after an extended break, the next level for you will likely be challenging, and that's okay. Like those before you, you can push through and emerge as the champion you are meant to be.

Overcome Your Doubts

Self-doubt, fear, frustration, and limiting beliefs in general are all very real and very understandable. They are familiar foes to me too, and they were the bullies that mocked and ridiculed me for over two decades when trying (and re-try-ing) to scale my business. Their words were harsh, and I took them as truths. I handed over my potential, my purpose, and my ability to serve at my highest level. They also stole the joy I knew I wanted and deserved—the joy that would come from helping others to dream, plan, and achieve their best. Then I decided **no more**.

Just three years ago, I decided it was my time to go from a successful but small consultancy to scaling my business, and that's when everything changed. More clients, more national podcast appearances, more Fortune 500 speaking engagements, more global workshops, and more joy. Please don't misunderstand me. These things did not fall from the sky. It was hard. I asked for (a lot of) help, and I was persistent. It took as long as eight months for some of my opportunities to materialize. The old Sheryl would have either 1) not tried, or 2) accepted the first 'no' (or second, third, or fourth) and quit. That was a tipping point for me and when I started going from dreaming to doing.

Doubt is like putting sugar in the tank of your car. It can slow momentum, and then cause progress to come to a complete standstill. I know what that feels like, and I'm passionate about making sure doubt doesn't get in the way of your next big win. World-class performers know how to be mentally tough, how to summon doubt and use it to fuel their success. You too can learn how to shake hands with doubt and take consistent bold action anyway.

ZONED IN Acceleration Exercise:

Please write one doubt you have about achieving your next level of ambition? Why must you overcome it now?

_____

_____

_____

_____

_____

Getting to Know Yourself

Gaining greater clarity around what you yearn for and why it's deeply important to you will be the foundation for your success. I've found that world-class athletes are remarkably clear about what they want and why, and it serves as a beacon for their success. According to *Forbes* writer and author of *Strategic Acceleration*, Tony Jeary, clarity should be your first priority.[3] If you've declared that it's your time, then the first step is getting crystal clear about what you want and why you care about it.

This *Get to Know Yourself Questionnaire* will help you next-level your understanding of who you are and what's important to you. You'll be looking from a perspective that may be unfamiliar, but this can be a catalyst to ignite momentum and inspire consistent action.

Here are a few important instructions to keep in mind, so you can get the most benefit from the questionnaire:

1. Make sure you're in a quiet place where you won't be disturbed by other people, pets, phones, watches, tablets, TV, etc. for 30 minutes. Feel free to answer a few questions at a time if you have less time in each sitting. It's important that you are 100% undistracted. If possible, play your favorite music while you're filling out this questionnaire.

2. Be honest. This task is not judged or graded. It's simply for your reflection.

3. Think from a place of abundance, not from a place of lack. Start flexing the muscle of optimism and infinite possibilities.

Get to Know Yourself Questionnaire

1. Are there any people or life events that have greatly impacted you? If so, how did they make you think, or what did they make you wonder about?

2. Without thinking about it too much, what makes you smile? What makes you happy? What makes you proud of yourself?

3. If you were sitting across the table from your best and most successful self (as defined by you), what would that self tell you right now?

4. By making progress towards your best self, who else will it impact?

5. If you were given three months to take action or your dream would vanish forever, how would you feel?

6. What do you consider your strengths that you most enjoy?

7. If you were going to make a huge request and ask someone for help, who would that be?

8. Why would this be important in getting what you want and deserve?

9. Why haven't you done it yet?

10. Imagine yourself standing on the top of a mountain with a magic wand, looking up at the top of a neighboring, much bigger mountain where the future you is standing. If you could wave a magic wand to transform your future self into the highest and happiest version of you, what would your highest and happiest self have accomplished and how would she feel?

11. When you are taken from this world, what do you want to be remembered for, and why is it important to you?

An Example Questionnaire

I've had the pleasure of working with a senior-level project manager in Silicon Valley for well over a year. Although we discuss her work, her primary focus is having a world-class relationship with her teenage daughter before she heads off to college in two years.

For anyone who has, or has had, a teenager—parenting means you need to be mentally tough, control your own emotions, and not get stuck on the emotional roller-coaster with them. It requires us to be patient and understanding, riding out the wave of them pushing us away and trying to prove they don't need us anymore, then their fear and frustration of knowing they still really do. This conflict often results in crying, door slamming, and yelling, and we must be mentally tough to love, guide, and support our teenagers through this time when they are not 100% human.

Here are the project manager's answers to this questionnaire. These answers may give you a different perspective on how heightened clarity, a plan, and world-class mental toughness helped this senior project manager in Silicon Valley, who is also a wife and mother.

1. Are there any people or life events that have greatly impacted you? If so, how did they make you think, or what did they make you wonder about?

   I was raised to work hard and do my best. It's part of me and important for me to live into this value. It makes me happy when I am contributing at my highest level. As for my relationship with my daughter, it stems from the fact that I was not particularly close to my mother. I wanted to create a bond with my daughter that I did not have with my mother. I need that, but my mindset and habits were not contributing to that goal.

2. Without thinking about it too much, what makes you smile? What makes you happy? What makes you proud of yourself?

   Helping my team and other teams that I am not expected to help and seeing their success makes me happy. At home, having a conversation with my daughter where we bond and connect makes me feel a high level of joy.

3. If you were sitting across the table from your best and most successful self (as defined by you), what would that self tell you right now?

   I would prepare for every important conversation and to give my full presence. The main problem was that I didn't know the importance of preparing for crucial conversations, and I certainly did not know how to have an influential mindset to be able to do it.

4. By making progress towards your best self, who else will it impact?

   It would impact me because I would be happier, but it would also impact my daughter. I am serving as a role model to her on how to persevere when something gets difficult and how to use my thoughts and emotions to my advantage and not to my detriment.

5. If you were given three months to take action or your dream would vanish forever, how would you feel?

   Not good. I would start planning a big trip with my daughter, and start figure out what legacy I want to leave at my work. The days are so busy, I'd lose sight of what's important to me and why. Then I'd look up, and months (or years) would have passed with no or little progress.

6. What do you consider your strengths that you most enjoy?

   I most enjoy problem solving, community, and connection.

7. If you were going to make a huge request and ask someone for help, who would that be?

   I'd ask for a meeting with the CEO of our company to better understand his initiatives and how I can best contribute. That sounds scary, but I know it's something I want to do.

8. Why would this be important to getting what you want and deserve?

    So, I can live into my best self by being clear on how I can best serve my company.

9. Why haven't you done it yet?

    I am afraid to ask.

10. Imagine yourself standing on the top of a mountain with a magic wand, looking up at the top of a neighboring, much bigger mountain where the future you is standing. If you could wave a magic wand to transform your future self into the highest and happiest version of you, what would your highest and happiest self have accomplished and how would she feel?

    I would have created a mentorship program at work to help young women in technology, and I would feel a great sense of joy and contribution. I am starting to realize how important this is to me, and it's making me less overwhelmed by what it will take to get started.

11. When you are taken from this world, what do you want to be remembered for, and why is it important to you?

    I want to be remembered by my family, colleagues, and community as kind, generous, patient, and caring.

ZONED IN Acceleration Exercise:

After answering the questions in your *Get to Know Yourself Questionnaire*, state one perspective that you didn't think of before, or one thing that nudged you in the direction of progress.

_____

_____

_____

_____

_____

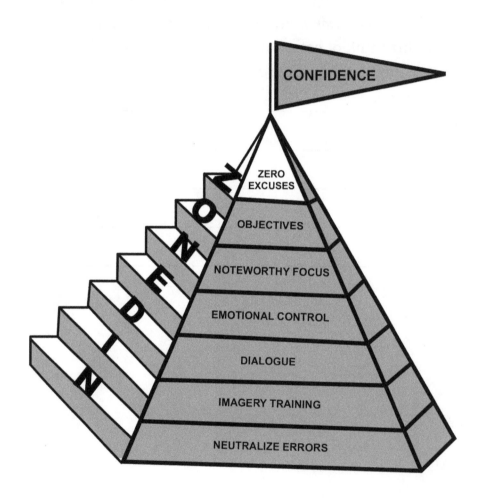

Chapter 2

ZERO EXCUSES

Setting up Your Structure for Success

"You may encounter many defeats,
but you must not be defeated." – Maya Angelou

My dad always used to say "There are no guarantees except death and taxes." Growing up, that saying made no sense, but now it does. When world-class athletes set their sights on the Olympics, there are no guarantees they will make it there—let alone make it onto the podium. I've had the opportunity to ask Olympic hopefuls and former Olympians what it was like the moment they decided to go for it. To go "all in." All of them said essentially the same thing: it was like "tunnel vision" when they decided, and there was no turning back. Then they had *zero excuses* on their quest to be the best. You can learn to have zero excuses too, so you can be "all in" and keep making progress even when there is no guarantee of success.

Before moving forward effectively, it's time to gain an important perspective and make peace with any past inaction, so you can be free of it going forward, so that's what we'll cover in this chapter. Then you'll learn a couple different ways to set up a solid accountability structure for yourself or for your team.

The Contribution and Cost of Inaction

If you are like most people (me included), you have started and stopped a passion project. Something that you knew would complete you. Something that was nagging at you like a sore tooth. Something that only kept away because you were too busy to allow it into your consciousness. Something that only knocked on your conscious when the world slowed down for a moment.

Maybe you entertained the thought briefly, ventured towards the door of success, or even got close but never quite made it. It's time to acknowledge that you did the best you could at the time and make peace with that chapter of your life. It's time to ask yourself: what is different *now*, and why must I move forward *now?*

Every time we don't work on that important thing, there is a cost of our inaction. Sometimes there is a contribution of inaction too, and it is not just valid and OK, but important. Maybe it was to fund you being able to take care of yourself, or your family, or some other reason. If that is the case, you must accept this cost and be at peace with it. If not, this past inaction will be a tack on your journey forward.

But, is your time now? Are you ready to work on something important to you? If so, ask yourself, what is the cost of inaction if you don't make progress *now*?

 ## ZONED IN Acceleration Exercise:

Write one reason why you haven't taken action (up to now) on an important ambition. Then add "which I accept as history, and I'm ready to commit to now."

_____

_____

_____

_____

_____

The Mindset Shift That Can Change Everything

You might be wondering why we need to make peace with previous inaction. Well, it's because life can sometimes be complex when it comes to being the best parent, spouse, friend, business owner, or employee we can be. Maybe we were tending one bucket and the others were put on hold. Maybe it truly was not your time to learn the mental toughness tools to take consistent bold action. Whatever the reason, it's important to set your sights on the person you want to become or on the ambition you yearn to achieve. Learning how to be mentally tough will help you focus your thoughts and your actions on where you are going and not where you've been. Making peace with previous inaction is like an Olympian who underperformed because she didn't train hard enough or because there were other circumstances demanding her attention. This peace will allow her to be free to train again, so she can emerge as a champion.

I've had to do this myself. Full transparency, I've had this business idea in me to help thousands reach their potential and to experience optimal joy in the process *for 20 years*! I started a couple times, but it got hard. Really hard. So, I quit. Then, for many years, I considered myself a failure at business. I had a small practice helping a handful of elite athletes and business professionals realize their potential and joy, but not on a scale that I dreamed about. That mindset encouraged me to almost give up, again.

I took a moment to reflect on what was happening at the time I labeled myself a 'failure' in business. In 1995, my father and rock to my somewhat dysfunctional, unstable family was diagnosed with stage 4 lung cancer. "Wait a minute," I had thought. "Who will take care of my mom who has severe bipolar disease and my brother, who although 10 years my senior, is struggling with addiction and being self-sufficient?" Most anxiety-producing, *who could I turn to?* Who would provide answers to all of the tough questions I had? Who would I turn to when life got hard? Who would show me the light of optimism and assure me that it would not just be okay, but *great*? Who could I lean on when everything around me was crumbling? Finally, who would be my biggest cheerleader for my triumphs, big and small?

At the age of 71, my father passed away. It was August 5, 1995, and I was five months pregnant with my first son, Dan. I was angry, sad, devastated, and lost. Shortly after Dan came his brother Ryan and sister Megan. I had three beautiful, healthy children under the age of six, but the lack of sleep and the energy required felt unmanageable at the time. I was also looking after my mom. Gradually, I found myself moving from survival mode (i.e. brushing my teeth, having an occasional shower, and taking care of three young children) to eventually sleeping a little more, getting some help with my kids and my mom, and feeling more joy in being a partner, parent, and friend.

I was also transitioning from leaning on my rock—my dad— to being the rock of my growing family. As a child, my father held our family together, helping my mother manage her bi-polar disorder and guiding my brother. I leaned on my father when I had a question, when I had a bad day, and when I needed advice. Now, I became to everyone else what my father was to me. It's a role that I have now accepted with pride and grace, a lot of willingness to ask for help, and an occasional cry, wishing I still had my dad to seek council from and lean on.

At that time, I couldn't have managed a full-time career and caring for my then small children and my mother. I have the deepest admiration and respect for those who are amazing parents while managing a career and/or caring for a loved one. But sometimes, we must realize our limitations, allocate our focus, and honor ourselves for where we are or where we have been.

I could not have been my best at both work and home when my kids were young. It took me a while to realize *that was okay*. In fact, it was more than okay. It's hard to exactly measure the dividends of spending a lot of focused time with my kids, who are now adults. I don't know how much of their achievements, happiness, and contribution are attributed to me or to their innate ability and personality. But I do know how priceless all of that time and effort was to me.

Is your cost of inaction in one area of your life a valid contributor to a greater cause like being fully present with your family, or do you have the bandwidth for more? Is the cost of inaction holding you back from your next big win? Maybe it's time to go small and do that well, or maybe it's time to dream and achieve on a grander scale. Either way, if you've decided it's time to live into your next level of ambition, your cost of inaction could be lack of progress, lack of serving others who need you or your knowledge, and/or the personal joy that comes from contributing to something bigger than yourself, something *you know you must do.*

ZONED IN Acceleration Exercise:

How have you been a little hard on yourself? What mindset shift do you need to break free of it?

_____

_____

_____

_____

_____

Your Support Team

"Growth is never by mere chance; it is the result of forces working together."

— James Cash Penny

Before you move forward to learn more about mental toughness, let's clear a path to success. Have you ever tried to get fit or lose weight with a pantry full of sugary carbohydrate-laden goodies? A better idea may be to get rid of the treats and stock the refrigerator with pre-cut fruits and vegetables and other healthy snacks. Maybe you have a significant financial goal, but you're spending time and money with friends, family, or colleagues who are living a different financial lifestyle. The same goes for laying the foundations to next-level any of your ambitions. In other words, it's important to *set yourself up for success.*

We all have great intentions, and often we know what to do to scale our business, get to the next level at work, or get into the best shape of our lives. Unfortunately, common sense is not always common action. In other words, we don't always do what we know we should do. We want something so badly, yet we don't consistently put in the work required to get there.

As we move through life, our ambitions change, and different ones rise up and ask for our attention. Personally, as my kids needed me less, I started to scale my business, and I had to seek an entirely new board of directors (i.e. coaches and mentors) to help me. I consumed books and online courses, went to live events, and joined ambitious and compassionate masterminds. My father always said that we are lifelong learners (which sounded awful as a young person!). Now, that makes sense, and I fully understand why we must commit to keep learning and growing.

But how do we put a system in place to ensure we are making consistent progress towards our biggest dreams and aspirations *in a holistic way*, rather than just focusing on one bucket at a time? How can we turn common sense into common action? The simple answer is, we need help.

The most successful people in the world surround themselves with people who inspire, guide, and collaborate with them, and keep them accountable. Henry Ford, for example, was fully aware that he wasn't the smartest person on his team. He knew what his vision was, then he found a team of engineers and business people who would complement his aspirations, passion, and work ethic to make his dream come true[5]. Similarly, the Wright brothers were two people who believed their dream of flight was possible, who crafted a team to help bring their dream to life, and who never gave up on that dream.

The examples in history are endless, but I'd also like to share one that's less well-known.

Wilma Rudolph was one of 22 children. She was born in 1940, and had a host of medical problems as a child including polio, an illness nearly eradicated today. It attacks the central nervous system, often causing developmental problems in children.[5] Wilma was told by her doctor at a very young age that she would never walk again. But Wilma's mother told her that she most certainly *would* walk again. Wilma decided to believe her mother.

Her journey began in a wheelchair and then with braces on her legs as a child. Wilma dreamed of being a "normal" kid who could someday play a sport. She just wanted to fit in. What many take for granted was a grueling journey for her.

To defy the odds and the limitations placed on her body, she faced a daily trek through pain, embarrassment, and setbacks.

However, she had an expert coach on character and determination (her mother) who believed in her and wouldn't let her quit. She also had a group of teammates (21 siblings) who were there to pick her up when she (literally) stumbled and fell. Wilma eventually gathered the strength and confidence to try out for the Burt High School basketball team in her freshman year. But, after her courage in asking the head coach to put her on the team and agreeing to work with him for 10 minutes a day every day before school, she got cut. Eventually, she made the team, mainly because the coach wanted Wilma's sister Yolanda to play. Their father agreed to let Yolanda play on the team, but only if Wilma could play too.

Through hard work and determination, certainly not because of G-d given talent or physical prowess, Wilma earned her spot on the high school basketball team roster. Wilma was then discovered by the track coach at the high school. He convinced her to try track and field, and soon became her expert coach.

In 1956, Wilma sprinted her way to a bronze medal at the Olympics in Melbourne aged just 16 and eventually won three gold medals in 1960 in Berlin. She tied the world record in the 100 meters and set a new Olympic record in the 200 meters. What's more, she brought her 400-meter relay team from behind to win gold![6]

Wilma proceeded every day as if her Olympic dream was possible and served as a role model for many women after her, most notably three-time gold medalist Jackie Joyner-Kersee, who ranked among the all-time greatest athletes in the heptathlon and long jump.[7]

Where would Wilma have been if her mother had agreed with the doctor? What if Wilma's mother had confined her to the wheelchair assigned to her? What if she'd discouraged Wilma from dreaming, planning, and achieving her best? If she hadn't helped Wilma dream of a future she couldn't yet see.

We always need someone to go to bat for us, like Wilma's parents and her track coach did for her. Someone to believe in us when sometimes we don't believe in ourselves. *Who is going to bat for you?* If no one is going to bat for you, **I am**. So please keep reading.

Your Expert Mentor/Coach

We must set ourselves up for success, and to do that, we often need an expert to help us achieve our goals. If you're trying to get fit, you might hire a trainer—someone who knows how to help you and who you are accountable to. You may need this structure until your exercise routine becomes a habit.

At work, if you're trying to climb the ladder, it's imperative that you have a mentor to push and challenge you, and support you when you feel defeated. We all feel defeated at different points in our lives, and that's okay. But once we become mentally tough, we are primed to receive the guidance from someone who has walked our path before us, and we are ready to take consistent action even if it's awkward or difficult at first.

You might be surprised who is willing to step up, but they may not tap you on the shoulder and offer. It's important be proactive and persistent when asking for help even if you think the answer might be no. While studying, researching, and learning from legendary athletes and business professionals, I've heard over and over again that the most successful people in the world ask for help—frequently.

According to K. Anders Ericsson, internationally acclaimed researcher and the world's leading expert on the science of expertise, "Real experts seek out constructive, even painful feedback. They're also skilled at understanding when and if a coach's advice doesn't work for them."[8]

If it isn't possible to hire an exercise professional, personal development specialist, or any other type of coach as your expert mentor/coach, then you may have to get creative. Here are a few tips:

- Use YouTube videos, books, or online courses as your coach or mentor.

- Declare to the world what you desire and the steps you are taking to get there. Hearing your objectives out loud and sharing them with a friend, colleague, or family member can be powerful motivation for you to take consistent action.

- Set up positive rewards when you learn from your "coach." For example, every day that you show up 30 minutes early to work to practice for your presentation, take a short walk after, or grab a "not too sugary" drink from a coffee shop.

- Set up negative consequences for yourself if you fail to practice. Do you strongly dislike cleaning up after the dog or organizing the garage? Let your family know that you'll be on the hook if you don't do X, Y, or Z.

Whether your coach is a mentor, your manager at work, a professional coach, or a YouTuber, it's vital that you engage with an expert, someone who is more experienced than you, and who has been where you want to go. That way, you will grow and improve.

 ## *ZONED IN Acceleration Exercise:*

- Who can offer you expertise on what you want to achieve?

- Will it be a leader or mentor at work?

- Will you hire a coach?

- Will you get creative and find a way to get some-one to help you? What's the worst that can happen if you do ask?

- What are the consequences if you don't?

Write three possibilities here and when you will take action:

_____

_____

_____

_____

Your Peer Accountability Partner

Sometimes, engaging a mentor or coach can be difficult, or we don't meet with them often enough to see the trans-formation we want and deserve, which can lead to delayed progress. Enlisting a peer, colleague, or friend as a cheer-leader can be a great way to boost motivation and create a sense of urgency between coaching or mentoring sessions, banishing those excuses.

Although this type of accountability is hands-down better than no accountability at all, ideally it should be *in addition to* a mentor, coach, or leader's accountability, not instead of.

We need the *expert* instruction of a mentor or leader to guide us—plus this cheerleader (or team of cheerleaders) who will have those difficult conversations with us when our effort isn't matching our ambition. And the more often, the better. Early on, a weekly or better yet daily check-in would be ideal.

So, how do we use a cheerleader accountability buddy to ensure zero excuses? The answer lies in social influence theory.

What is Social Influence Theory and How Can We Use It?

Social influence is basically what it sounds like, a change in a person's behavior that is caused by another person or group of people. This change can come about intentionally or unintentionally. Either way, the behavior change is based on how the person perceives themselves in relationship to the influencer, or even to society in general.[9] Once you understand the three different types of social influence, you can use this theory to your advantage to eliminate excuses and help you stay accountable.

Harvard professor of social ethics and psychologist Herbert Kelman identified three general areas of social influence[10]:

1. **Compliance:** As human beings, we tend to adhere to social pressure and have an internal drive for compliance. If the social pressure is good, such as a colleague helping you with a presentation, then you're more likely

to "comply," and put in more effort than you would on your own.

We can use this internal drive for compliance when forming new habits or working towards a desired yet difficult result, such as exercising or public speaking, by asking an appropriate peer, colleague, or friend to help us out. Maybe you dread waking up early or the pain it takes to initially get in shape. However, you'll do it *if* you have someone that you're accountable to. We comply by showing up, not letting our accountability buddy down.

2. **Identification:** This takes place when we are influenced by someone who is liked and respected. Whether it's our personal wellness, climbing the ladder at work, or some other endeavor, our behaviors can change based on *who* we are accountable to. If you choose someone who you would *like* to identify with, you'll be paving the way for progress. However, this can backfire if you pick the wrong person, so it's important to carefully choose who you identify with, and how and consider why you identify with them.

   When doing this, specifically who do you identify with? This identification can be all-encompassing, or not. For example, you may choose an accountability buddy to help you become a better presenter at work. This person may be dedicated to their eating, sleeping, and exercise routine. On top of that, they may have strong family and community relationships that are consistently being nurtured and improved. In other words ... you could identify with them all round.

Or perhaps you choose an amazing business person who doesn't have the other habits that are ideal for you. That's okay *if* you are only seeking social support in business, and you do not feel the need to align with someone who has health, wellness and relationship habits that are important to you. However, it's worth remembering "You are the average of the FIVE people you spend the most time with" (Jim Rohn), so choose your people wisely. In the next section, we'll look at how to do that.

3. **Internalization:** This means that individuals accept influence, either publicly or privately, because the behavior is *inwardly* rewarding (i.e. it makes them feel proud or happy). In these cases, we are motivated intrinsically to make progress even if the process is challenging. This internalization also occurs when a behavior aligns with our value system. Of course, to use this to our advantage, we must be intimately aware of what our value system is. What are your beliefs? What is your philosophy? What standards are important for you to live by?

Internalization can help us when we experience growing pains, which happens often. In these times, we must be vulnerable and willing to embrace being uncomfortable. Internalization is the cheerleader that will pull you through when the journey gets challenging and you want to surrender. It will also provide the extra push inches before the finish line when you feel like you can't take another step.

When we create this type of accountability structure for ourselves, we essentially construct a system to influence ourselves to move towards our best selves. Regardless of how we are influenced, it's important to raise our sense of awareness and set up a structure for our success.

How To Choose and Work With An Accountability Buddy

As we saw, it's important to choose the right buddy for accountability structure to work effectively. If you do, it can help you become the champion you are meant to be. So how do you choose the right peer, friend, or colleague as an accountability buddy? Well, they should be:

- ❏ More experienced than you (ideally)
- ❏ Have your best interests at heart
- ❏ Not in competition with you in any way
- ❏ Not threatened by you

It's also important to take care of some housekeeping early on. Here are a few important things to discuss prior to getting started with an accountability buddy:

- **Be explicit** about what is important to you, what you are committed to doing, and what help you are hoping for. If you ask someone and they aren't fully on board, that's okay. Thank them for their honesty and for considering it, then move on.

- **Ensure they are committed to the process.** For example, will they show up consistently? When will you meet and what time? Be very transparent at the outset about how important this process is to you.

- **Verbally commit** to practicing/teaching as soon as possible after you've received guidance from an expert. Let your accountability buddy know what you are practicing and when this will happen. By committing out loud to them, you are committing to yourself. You may want to schedule a specific time with your accountability buddy to "teach" them what you've learned.

- **Commit to the process and to progress**, rather than the outcome. It will allow you to pivot when needed and be as agile as possible, especially when setbacks occur. We'll talk about setbacks in

Chapter 5, but for now, accept that failure is an important part of getting better. Communicate this to your accountability buddy, so that both of you share the same philosophy.

This type of accountability structure will help you have zero excuses—even when the climb gets hard. As I'm sure you've experienced, the next level of success almost always gets difficult. The good news is that you can create a structure for your success. When you get knocked down (and you will—it's almost as sure as death and taxes!) you'll have a cheerleader there to help you dust off and get back in your arena of personal success.

According to Navy SEAL and *Forbes* contributor Brent Gleeson, accountability breeds excellence and ensures ownership.[11] It's easy to see how accountability can affect your behavior. But to get more accountability in your life, you must be consistent to get consistent results. If you want to change your behavior and achieve beyond your current circumstances, it's time to choose and commit to a peer, colleague, or friend who will serve as your accountability buddy. Will you be theirs too?

ZONED IN Acceleration Exercise:

List three friends or colleagues who might serve as good accountability buddies for you.

_____

_____

_____

_____

Self-Accountability

All forms of accountability are important and serve a purpose on our quest to be our best. Self-accountability is the anchor we must drop to rise above the rest to find our highest source of accomplishment and joy. It's in those quiet moments—when you go to bed, when you wake up, at the track when no one is around, or when you get to work very early—that you must depend on yourself to have accountability and zero excuses. It's what no one else is willing to do that helps our greatest success move from dream to reality.

YOU are your best ally.

Many times, you know what to do, but your progress is pushed aside for other projects and other people's needs. If you're like me, you're a giver, which is fantastic! But this can also be to your detriment *if* you don't know how to prioritize what's important to you. The result? You continue to make progress on what's important to you, consistently.

I'm not saying disregard family obligations or commitments at work, but it may be time to set some boundaries. This section will teach you how to find time for what matters, and how to protect it. The process of self-accountability is similar to what was outlined in the last two sections but it requires an extra step.

This is how to create an accountability structure for yourself:

1. **Secure time with yourself.**

    When your best friend, family member, or child needs you, are you there? What about a doctor's appointment that has been in your calendar for months? Do you cancel on a whim or if it's inconvenient? Probably not. It's time to start making appointments with yourself that are just as important and that you are just as committed to.

2. **Write your commitment down.**

    There is one simple way of making those small successes more likely. Ideally, place your written commitment somewhere that you will see it often, such as in your calendar on the wall, a note on your computer or on your mirror in your bathroom.

3. **Socialize it.**

   For example, tell a neighbor and your family that you will be going to the gym on Monday, Wednesday, and Friday mornings. Practicing your presentation at work? Tell your colleagues that you will be in the conference room from 12:00 to 12:20 p.m. every day this week. You get the idea.

4. **Raise the importance.**

   Do you work out simply to look good, or do you want to be around as long as possible for your kids? Are you striving to scale your business, get that raise to make more money or provide for a loved one, or maybe take a trip that will create lasting memories? Get detailed about why you care so deeply, not just the surface reasons.

Challenge yourself

A coach's job is to teach, cheerlead, *and* challenge. Great coaches do just that. They push their students beyond their comfort zone. Science says this is a vital component of making progress and becoming and expert.[12] Whether you have a coach or not, it's vital that you learn to challenge yourself. A challenge makes us sit up and take notice, helps us focus on a task, and can give us the confidence to move forward even when it's hard or scary.

Often, taking on a new ambition can be exciting and down-right frightening at first. When I got asked to speak at a large venue, I almost declined the first time because I was so scared! It's not just us that gets scared though. Even world-class ath-letes and CEOs get scared in certain contexts. Being able to challenge yourself is a way of saying "You can do this!" even if you're frightened or unsure. Here are a couple ways to chal-lenge yourself, so you can stay accountable:

- **Take on bite-size pieces.** Your challenges should be controllable tasks that are most important for your long-term success. For example, if you want to pivot in your career, you may challenge yourself to research and reach out to five companies, even if they're companies you think you have no chance of being hired. Consider that there's a 100% chance of failure if you don't try.

- **Set a deadline for your challenge.** For example, reach out to those companies in the next 24 hours.

- **Pause when you reach your deadline.** Do not immediately move on to the next task. If you were successful, great! Time to celebrate. If not, reas-sess, reset your challenge, and set your new dead-line. What did you learn and what will help you succeed on the next leg of your journey?

Self-accountability is a tool to develop over time, ideally once you have the knowledge, support, and consistency gained from an expert to make progress on your own. If you're ready to jump in, let's do it!

ZONED IN Acceleration Exercise:

What steps can you take to set up an accountability structure for yourself? When will you secure time to practice and make progress? How will you challenge yourself?

_____

_____

_____

_____

_____

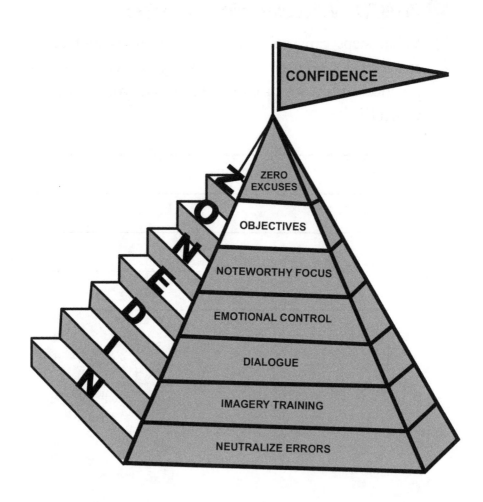

Chapter 3

OBJECTIVES

Charting a Path for
Where You Want to Go

"I know how it looks. But just start. Nothing is insurmountable." – Lin-Manuel Miranda

Now that you've reassessed your ambitions, know what you want to next-level, and have a structure in place to ensure zero excuses, it's time to put a plan in place. Without a plan, we are left with a fleeting wish that gets interrupted incessantly by life, whose enemy is time, and whose success is eventually denied. Planning our objectives carefully and fluidly is vital, because lack of clarity breeds randomness, which is a recipe for inaction or misguided action.

When an Olympian has a big dream, their plan might include specific skills to improve, a clear training regimen every day, competitions during the year, and time to reflect on their journey to victory. You can create a plan like this too. Our ship needs to know where to sail, and we must believe the destination isn't so remote that we'll never get there. In this chapter, we're going to chart the path for where you want to go.

Your Long-term Objective: Key Component to Dreaming BIG

We'll start with the end in mind, discuss why this is important, and how to dream big. If we can get clarity on what we yearn for, we'll be able to see what course of action to take. And when we can see it, we'll be able to believe it and take consistent action towards it. Why is clarity important you might ask? Whether it's lack of clarity about our long-term ambitions or the most important tasks for the day, I've found that being unclear is kryptonite to our productivity *and* joy.

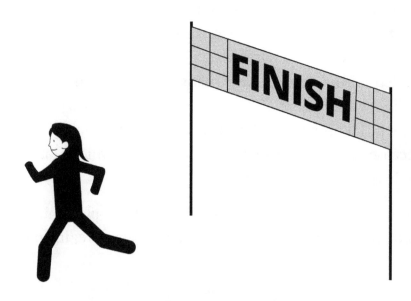

I've experienced this personally and seen it in countless individuals and organizations. Whether it's clarity on any given day, for a project, or on a long-term mission, clarity is more important than you may realize. Planning for your next level of ambition is like starting a race from the finish line, from your long-term objective.

While writing this book, I spent a lot of time in one of my favorite places: Sonoma, California. It's in the heart of wine country, just north of San Francisco. I'd wake up before sunrise and head to the Overlook Trail, which zig-zags through trees, streams, and pastures until it ends at a brick bench overlooking the entire Sonoma Valley. On one of my trips, I took a wrong turn on the way down and found myself in the neighboring cemetery. It was beautiful and eerie at the same time.

Time slowed, and then it stopped.

I became aware of those who were not in a rush. The residents of the cemetery whose gift was either realized or denied.

In that moment, I slowed down and asked: *What is my dream? What will be written on my grave stone? How will I be remembered? Whose lives will I have touched and in what way? How will I leave this place better than when I arrived? When I am asked to give my gift back, will I be satisfied and at peace that I have done it justice?*

How about you?

At some point, you will be called to give back the gift placed inside you. When that day comes, let's make sure you are ready, knowing you gave it your best effort. If you want to fully grasp this concept, take a trip to your local cemetery like I did, and spend a little time there. I didn't see it as depressing. I saw it as a gentle (or not so gentle) reminder that our time here is limited. A reminder that we must commit to consistent progress, and that perfection is a villain who will only get in our way. There is no more time for fear, doubt, and procrastination.

Slowing down and taking a moment to be still with our own truths takes a certain level of dedication, commitment, and bravery. It's not easy, so don't forget that you are already world-class for taking it on.

ZONED IN Acceleration Exercise:

1. Take 30 minutes to be still and 100% uninterrupted by devices, people, pets, etc.

2. Imagine you are in a cemetery with beautiful trees, flowers, and various headstones.

3. Write or audio-record your own eulogy of what was important to you, what you accomplished, and what your gift was. How would you want it to read? Are you smiling with pride and fondness?

_____

_____

_____

_____

_____

4. Read this to someone you trust and respect or read it aloud to yourself.

Dream Big and Smart

When you're setting your destination, and charting your next move, it's important to think *big*. You might have heard that goals should be S.M.A.R.T., but the magic really happens when we dream big and smart. Think about it. Dr. Martin Luther King Jr. had a dream, not a carefully planned S.M.A.R.T. goal! Steve Wozniak had a dream of a personal computer in the 1970s when his Hewlett Packard colleagues couldn't figure out why anyone would want to carry around a computer. They couldn't see Wozniak's personal computing dream. Roger Bannister had a dream of running a sub-four-minute mile before anyone else had done it, and he did it in 1954. The list of "crazy" dreams that have come to life in history is endless.

Maybe you're not aiming for world peace and equality, revo-lutionizing a marketplace, or setting a world record, but make sure your dream is big enough. Grant yourself permission to dream BIG. Then, make your dream as vivid and visceral as possible. What would it feel like to cross the finish line? What would it take? Who would you celebrate with?

However, do keep these guidelines in mind when setting your long-term objectives:

- **Six months to four+ years:** This is a general guideline, and not a hard and fast rule. You need enough time to see significant progress, but not so much time that your goal is too far out of reach.

- **Realistic or not**: Whether 100% attainable or highly unlikely, this objective should at a minimum be remotely possible. An example for me would be running a marathon in under five hours, which would be very attainable, while under four hours would be extremely unlikely, and under three hours would be virtually impossible.

- **Be at peace with having little to no control:** For example, getting a promotion. You don't have control over the final decision or who the competition will be. But that lack of control shouldn't stop you from putting in the work. Acknowledge the lack of control and whatever emotions come along with it, make peace with this lack of control, and then commit to moving forward anyway.

ZONED IN Acceleration Exercise:

What's the one thing you dream of, or have a strong desire to achieve in the next six months to four years? Why is your long-term objective important to you? Please ask yourself why at least three times or three layers down to discover your true *why*.

_____

_____

_____

_____

_____

Intermediate Objectives: Connecting Big Dreams to the NOW

Children are notorious dreamers. When my son Dan was in pre-school, he donned a cape every morning when he got to school, as did his friends. They were superheroes with powers that the other kids didn't have. They were going to protect the playground and save the world. That was their truth, and they "flew" around every recess setting the bullies right, dusting off the kids who fell, and offering words of encouragement to anyone who was frustrated or upset.

I'm not sure where or when we lose our superpowers. Our ability to wholeheartedly believe what we want and deserve is possible—that it's already ours. Maybe it's past failures or believing other people's negative or discouraging words as the truth. Well, it's time to put our capes on again—to get strategic and commit to progress.

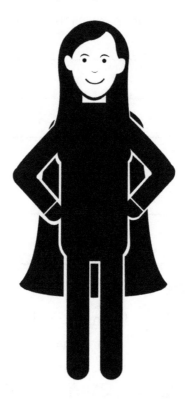

But what's the best way to make progress towards a long-term dream without losing motivation in the process? Once we truly believe that what we desire is possible, we become ready to close the gap between what we yearn for and actually achieving it. To do this, we need to set intermediate objectives.

Intermediate objectives provide some control and direction, so our ship knows where to sail without losing the power of the wind or going too far off-course. Intermediate objectives help us stay resilient and motivated on our path to getting what we want and deserve.

Keep in mind the following guidelines when setting intermediate objectives:

- **Two weeks to two months in duration:** Again, this is not a hard and fast rule, but you must have enough time to see improvement.

- **Limited control over accomplishment:** You'll have some control over your progress, but not complete control over your results. It's important to be at peace with this.

- **Quantifiable, so we can measure improvement:** These goals are driven by measuring our improvement, which is a great motivator and guide to help us be as agile as possible.

- **60-day review:** If we are on course, fantastic. Maybe we can accelerate a bit. If we are veering off or slowing down, we need to be aware of this too. Maybe we need additional help, new skills, or heightened awareness. This review will keep us on target.

You may have heard of different time frames for intermediate goals, but I intentionally keep these objectives on the shorter side. In my work with hundreds of high school, college, and world-class athletes, and business professionals, having a 60-day assessment of their skills has proven instrumental in accelerating their progress. In other words, we must be able to adapt on our quest from good to great.

In addition, 66 days is about the time it takes to form a habit.[13] Once we form a new habit, that skill set is near mastery, and we are ready to take on the next most important skill. This is ultimately how we become proficient. Without a 60-day review, we are at risk of decelerating progress by 1) practicing the wrong activity or 2) becoming detached from seeing improvement. Sixty days is a great length of time to drive momentum from our current course—or shift direction and adapt to meet our changing abilities.

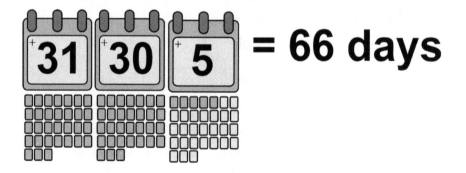

The power of progress

Progress is powerful. In a recent study of 7 companies that took place over 9–38 weeks, employees kept a diary of something that stood out in their minds each day. At the end of the study, 11,637 diaries were collected. The results? "The single best predictor of motivation was progress in meaningful work."[14]

It's imperative to set intermediate objectives that are congruent with our long-term dream, so we can monitor our progress. These objectives help us stay focused on the process of getting better—rather than the outcome of our efforts on our long-term dream. Intermediate objectives provide the feedback needed for us to be decisive and stay motivated when the work gets difficult.

When setting objectives, it's common to practice or complete what's easiest. I know I'm tempted to do this sometimes! However, we must not simply make the most common and comfortable choice. We must do what is the *most important*, which may be what is the most difficult. Yes, the process may be difficult or embarrassing, and you may not be an immediate success, but it's a habit worth forming if you are serious about your success.

It's just like a tennis player switching from a two-handed backhand to a one-handed backhand. Strokes get worse before they get better, and the mechanics often feel awkward. It may be a struggle at first. But if you're serious about being world-class at what matters most to you, it's time to roll up your sleeves and commit to improving. Make peace and accept any fear, doubt, or trepidation, and vow to move forward anyway. No one ever started at the top or was born with the skills to win a gold medal. You'll get there.

 ## ZONED IN Acceleration Exercise:

What is one technical skill you must improve to take your ambition to the next level? How do you currently rate yourself on a scale of one to ten? Where will you need to be in the next two weeks to two months?

For example: "In the next two months, it's most important that I improve in becoming a more engaging and impactful speaker. On a scale of one to ten, I would currently rate myself as a six. I am committed to becoming an eight in two months."

_____

_____

_____

_____

Short-Term Objectives: The Stepping Stones to Where You Want to Go

Striving for our highest level of performance is tough. Becoming world-class at what's important is less about perfection and talent and more about gaining clarity, confidence, and control over what matters most. Your reward? Motivation and increased self-efficacy (your belief in yourself) from the clarity and accomplishment that comes along with consistent progress.

Have you ever been to a baseball game? You know the many small stairs that lead up to the top of the stadium? Short-term objectives are the small necessary steps that, when done consistently, will get you to the top of the stadium (your long-term objective). But only if you focus on the process of putting one foot in front of the other rather than being too concerned with how far away the top of the stadium looks.

How short-term objectives help big dreams take shape

Back in 2010, Kimberly Bryant was an executive working in Silicon Valley for a large biotech company. Twenty years after she received her engineering degree from Vanderbilt University, the lack of progress for women in technology was not acceptable to Ms. Bryant. A year later, she started Black Girls Code to get young women aged 7 to 17 interested in programing, web design, and robotics.

Black Girls Code now offers courses in computer programming, electrical engineering, mobile app development, robotics, and other STEM fields and has grown to over 2,000 students within its first two years. It operates in many states across the U.S. and in Johannesburg, South Africa. It was the consistent and actionable steps that took this amazing accomplishment from an idea to changing the lives of young girls across the country.[15]

What enables pioneers like Kimberley Bryant and world-class athletes alike to make this steady progress to emerge as the champions of their dreams is in part their ability to achieve those small yet consistent short-term objectives. If you have a passion, are willing to put in the work consistently, and are willing to ask for help, you can get there too.

How to set short-term objectives

To create the small stepping stones that will help *you* make consistent progress, it's time to set some short-term objectives. What will motivate *you* to keep you going, to make that steady climb to the top of your mountain?

A few things to keep in mind when setting short-term objectives are:

- **Up to two weeks away:** These are short-term, actionable and controllable steps.

- **Total control:** Either you will do them, or you won't. They're 100% up to you, and not dependent on anyone else or any factors out of your control.

- **Possible:** Shoot for challenging, even uncomfortable, but still *possible* objectives.

- **Specific:** They are very detailed and specific on time, place, and the details of what you're going to do.

Rather, if you want to get into shape, short-term objectives would include the time, place, duration, and effort level you are committing to. For example, rather than "I'll start running," a better short-term objective would be "I'll run a 9:00-minute per mile pace for 30 minutes on Monday, Wednesday, and Friday before work from 6:30–7:00am." This specificity ensures tasks are not left to chance and gives you accountability. Once the objective is established, block it out in your calendar like an important appointment.

This short-term goal takes your long-term objective into consideration and focuses on the most important steps in your control, so you can make progress. In the near term, it's vital to focus on the controllable process of *improving* rather than the outcome of your efforts.

ZONED IN Acceleration Exercise:

When it comes to your short-term objectives, what are the two most important things that you have control over and that you must do consistently to improve in the next two weeks?

_____

_____

_____

_____

Common Mistakes When Setting Short-term Objectives

Short-term objectives are simple, but not always easy to accomplish. In fact, there are some common pitfalls to be aware of, such as objectives that are too vague, too easy, or too hard. Avoid these and you'll set yourself up for success and consistent progress.

When your short-term objectives are too vague, it's less likely that you will achieve them. If you want specific results, then set specific tasks with a detailed plan. Try to get an expert or a buddy's help to provide accountability, then set a specific practice schedule. For example, if you want to get fit, then talk to a fitness professional and arrange a detailed routine with them every week. If the gym doesn't sound appealing, ask your buddy to work out with you and schedule a convenient time to go running each week. If you need to practice for an upcoming presentation, the same buddy system applies.

Also avoid short-term objectives that are too easy or too hard. Doing what's easy consistently doesn't help you improve. Nor does attempting objectives that are too difficult or virtually impossible due to time or ability limitations. Allow a realistic amount of time to complete your short-term objectives, and ensure they are at a minimum remotely possible. It's great to push yourself, but it's important to be mindful of how far.

Keep these pitfalls and solutions in mind and you'll have a great shot at keeping up with the small but mighty steps toward your next big win.

 ## ZONED IN Acceleration Exercise:

How can you make your short-term objective specific, so you can have a better chance of getting it done? How might you celebrate each important small step after you achieve it?

_____

_____

_____

_____

How You Practice Matters

Geoff Colvin's book *Talent is Overrated* sums this up. Becoming world-class at what matters most is more about working hard and consistently than having natural talent, which Colvin proves through many examples and research. Success, however you define it, is less about talent and more about how much you believe in—and how hard you work toward—what you yearn for. However, working hard and putting in hours is not enough on its own. We must also practice in a certain way.

In K. Anders Ericsson's *PEAK: Secrets from the New Science of Expertise*, Ericsson explains that 10,000 hours of practice is important, but it's not just about putting in the hours. How we structure our practice on our quest to be our best is extremely important too. And he's spent the better part of three decades researching and proving this.

If you want to accelerate your progress towards what you dream about and what you yearn for, you need to *practice deliberately*. Once you've identified relevant short-term objectives, practicing them deliberately is a powerful way to accelerate progress and stay highly motivated along the way.

So, what does deliberate practice mean? In Chapter 2, we looked at the impactful research compiled by Ericsson on the importance of having a mentor, coach, manager, or expert to guide you along the way, push you beyond your comfort zone, and help you attempt activities beyond your current level of competency.

Once you get this input or advice, Ericsson explains that it's important to practice as soon as possible. If you don't have a peer, coach, manager, or mentor, then get some input from an outside source, possibly ask a trusted and compassionate friend of family member. I am confident you will find someone (if you are persistent) to help you push beyond your limits. Then practice do what you learn as soon as you can after you learn it.

Ericsson also stresses the importance of *focused* practice rather than diluted or distracted practice. For example, when practicing for a presentation, it's best to set aside time that is void of all interruptions from colleagues, devices etc. This may require a little planning such as turning off notifications and putting a note on the door. If you are not part of the minuscule percentage of people who are good at multi-tasking, it's best to make what precious time you have to prepare as valuable as possible.

Focused practice also means choosing exactly what is most important to work on. For public speaking, is it tone, energy, content, gestures, etc.? Practicing one aspect at a time is more concentrated, while doing a general run through is more diluted. It's also very important to build a skill by strategically adding different aspects of that skill. Let's go back to the tennis player for example. If the 80% of the serves are going into the service box, then it's time to move on to aiming for a specific part of the service box. Similarly, if you have mastered the content for a pitch, it may be time to work on your energy, confidence, or inflection points. This gives each practice session the goal of improving, rather than just practicing without a specific end in mind.

As proven over the last 35 years of research with world-class athletes, musicians, chess players, and many other experts, learning how to practice deliberately can help all of us champion our results.

 ## ZONED IN Acceleration Exercise:

What is the most important skill you need to improve now, and how will you practice deliberately?

_____

_____

_____

_____

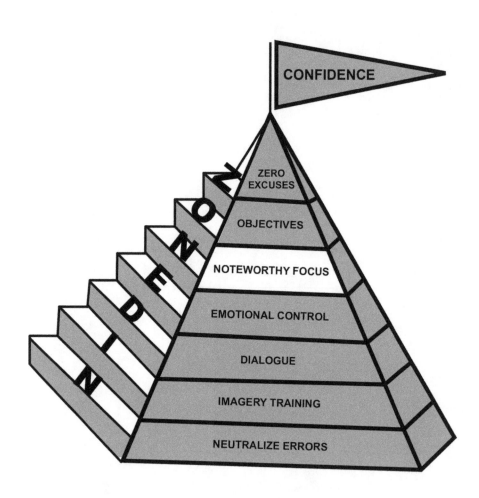

Chapter 4

NOTEWORTHY FOCUS

How to Accelerate Progress
and Take Control of Results

*"The successful warrior is the average man,
with laser-like focus." – Bruce Lee*

Suppose you're an Olympic downhill skier, waiting in the chute for the bull horn to blow and the gate to open. You've practiced for well over a decade for this moment. Then, your mind wanders towards an injury you suffered a year ago after a minor crash. For a moment, you ponder the possibility of not making it onto the podium, and wasting all the time, money, effort, and sacrifice from you and your family. The horn blows, the chute opens, you hesitate, and it's over. You weren't focused, so your dream slipped through your fingers even though you were capable and deserved to win. This chapter will help you make sure this never happens to you. It will help you own the moments that you've prepared hard for, so you can celebrate the joy that comes with giving 100%.

Moments Matter

Noteworthy focus is a vital tool you'll need to accelerate your progress during practice, and to lay down your best run when the stakes are high. You don't have to be an Olympian or take part in a world-class event to achieve noteworthy focus though. It might be that you're presenting a new idea to senior leaders, competing in your first race, or having a difficult yet crucial conversation with a family member. When the big moment comes, will you allow past events or future worries to derail the outcome you yearn for? Or, will you show up and feel the satisfaction and joy of knowing you did your absolute best?

Moments matter. I have witnessed how world-class athletes are laser focused during practice and during competition, to the point where they are barely even aware of the sights and sounds around them. I am certainly no Olympian, but I did practice for four years as a teen for a national equestrian show-jumping competition that I was capable of winning and very well-prepared for. The result? Failure, because I lost focus. That devastation stayed with me for many years, well into my career—that inability to level-up in those important moments.

'What if it happens again?' I thought, *'What if I'm really not good enough?'* Just like the downhill skier who thought about a past injury when waiting to start her race, my dream slipped through my fingers, even though I was capable and deserved to win. All because I didn't know how to focus. Don't let that be you. You work too hard not to show up and give your best in the most important moments.

Then there's those moments we take out from our busy schedule to prepare and practice for an important presentation, pitch, race, or conversation. Our focus in those preparation moments matters too. How do we maximize that precious practice time, so we can accelerate our proficiency? How did the downhill skier work over the past decade to prepare for the privilege of making it to the Olympics? She had to be focused in every moment that she dedicated to getting better. You can also learn how to focus in the moments dedicated to preparation, so you can make the most progress possible.

ZONED IN Acceleration Exercise:

What important event do you have coming up that you need to be laser-focused for when practicing? What potential distractions or worries could you have when you're practicing/preparing?

_____

_____

_____

_____

_____

Appropriate and Inappropriate Cues

Whether practicing or competing, we must first gain perspective on what triggers our behavior during practice and competition, so we can accelerate our progress and access what we are truly capable of.

Focus can be troublesome, especially these days when it's increasingly difficult to unplug or put on the blinders needed to monotask. It seems like notifications on our phones, watches, and computers are conditioning us to have ever shorter attention spans. However, being able to monotask is a key factor in focusing effectively during practice and competing against ourselves and others.

If we try to multitask, there are only so many thoughts that our minds can handle at one time. If we try to focus on more than one, our performance typically suffers. In fact, only 2% of people are effective multitaskers.[16] For the rest of us, me included, multitasking detracts from our focus on what matters most.

One way to focus when we're trying to become more proficient or during competing is to recognize our appropriate and inappropriate cues. In other words, we must be able to decipher which cues are important to focus on and which ones to ignore. Appropriate cue mastery enables us to improve and perform under pressure, so we can make the most of our practice time and concentrate on what matters most during competition.

I've found that many elite athletes report having very little awareness of their competition, surroundings, or other things out of their control. Instead, they are focused on the cues that trigger their next best move. For example, if your opponent starts bouncing the tennis ball before a serve, this cues a highly proficient tennis player to move her feet and get her racket up. An open field in soccer can be a cue for a player to accelerate and move into position.

You can also mentally set these cues for yourself. For example, every time you walk into a board room, you could touch the door jam, just like a football player touches the top of the player's tunnel before entering the field. As the conference room fills up, you could take five deep breaths, and focus on having eye contact with your colleagues. This is a way of taking control of your performance, so it doesn't control you.

If you practice this enough, whenever you enter the board room, you'll default to touching the door jam, taking five deep breaths, and having eye contact (or whatever controllable factor is most important in doing your best). You won't default to worry, doubt, or any other distractions. Walking into the board room will now be an appropriate cue to get laser-focused on what you can control to ensure the best possible outcome.

When we master appropriate cues in practice, we become more proficient, because we are moving from thinking and doing to *just doing*. This clears mental space to shift our attention to something else, which is how we can get better and better. For example, if a colleague asks you a question or challenges the data during your presentation, you will already have mastered how to get focused and have eye contact with them. This opens up mental space to answer the questions as intelligently and confidently as you can.

Think about it this way. When you first learned to walk as a child, you no doubt fell down a lot. But eventually, you could walk without too much thought. Then you went from walking to being able to run. Maybe you became a competitive runner, using the gun sounding as a cue to become balanced and relax your shoulders. At this point, you are so proficient that you can focus on ensuring an efficient stride and using your arms to generate momentum.

Inevitably, since you are human, the opposite also happens—inappropriate cues disarm your focus. This is an important obstacle to navigate, because the consequences of allowing inappropriate cues to undermine your practice or performance can be significant. Say your opponent is bouncing the tennis ball before serving to you. Instead of the positive cue "Move my feet," your cue may be a negative thought, "What if I lose the point again?" Then, you lose focus on what you must do to play well—moving your feet.

If inappropriate cues become our default, then our progress and performance can suffer. So, the next time you're preparing for an important meeting, presentation, or crucial conversation, it's important to establish appropriate cues, and learn how to recognize and replace the inappropriate ones.

ZONED IN Acceleration Exercise:

How can you create an appropriate cue when preparing for an important upcoming event? Do you have inappropriate cues that you need to replace? If so, please state what you will do to replace them.

_____

_____

_____

_____

_____

Adaptive Thinking

Now imagine you're an Olympic hopeful in a 400m track and field competition. After not just one but a string of significant losses, you still make it to the time trials. The top three in this meet qualify to move on from the trials, while the rest do not. Sprinting is your life, and the next few seconds will determine whether your dream lives or dies. The gun sounds. You get off to a good start, but you make a critical error in the first turn. What do you do to recapture your focus, so you can end up with a world-class performance? Do you use the error as an appropriate cue to regroup and give more, or as an inappropriate cue to give up or dwell on the error?

Whether you yearn to win a medal, get a raise, have an influential conversation, get your first client, or earn your first million, you *will* slip up, make mistakes, or miss a shot here and there. Everyone does, even senior leaders, world-class athletes, and yes, you too.

Adaptive thinking is a way to train your brain to be as agile as possible. This means that when an inevitable error happens, you'll be able to quickly recover your focus on what is most important for your best performance. Developing adaptive thinking doesn't guarantee a "W" every time, but it will certainly help you get on track, or back on track, to finish as strong as possible.

So, how can we foster more adaptive thinking to be as agile as possible when the unexpected happens? It all starts with understanding the difference between empirical facts and interpretations. This distinction is vital to perform at your best, because interpretations can be a strong driving factor in emotional reactions and behavior.[17]

Although it's not always a bad thing when interpretations drive our behavior (in fact, it's necessary at times), we must learn to filter the helpful interpretations from the detrimental ones. For example, when hiking, you see an agitated bear on the trail with her cubs. The empirical fact is that there's an angry bear on the trail. The interpretation is mainly DANGER and that she will eat you for lunch unless you surrender and retreat. This interpretation is extremely helpful and can save your life.

Often, however, we impose invalid and imaginary interpretations on ourselves, which can slow our progress and disable us in the moments that matter. Say you're preparing for an important interview, presentation, or pitch. There are key decision-makers at this meeting. That's an empirical fact. Your idea, product, or service may or may not be well-received, and you may get rejected all together. That is an interpretation configured in your own mind. It's *your* truth, but not *the* truth, because it hasn't happened yet.

Through your interpretation, you've created an inappropriate cue: "Important meeting = failure/rejection." But you're not on a hiking trail with an agitated bear who might attack you. You're in an important meeting where you need to devote your full attention to what you have control over.

If you don't filter your interpretations, the best-case scenario is that your thoughts are distracting, and you may be able to refocus on the controllable factors (we'll discuss how to do this in the next chapter). Worst-case scenario, the faulty interpretation triggers negative emotions that affect your behavior, leaving you unable to focus on what matters most.

You may enter the mouth of a downward spiral and create a self-fulfilling prophecy: "I knew it. My product/service/idea was not well-received, and I was rejected." How do you think this affects you the next time you're in a highly important situation? Just like concussions, the compound effect of this faulty logic can be harmful to your future performance.

When you learn to filter your interpretations into appropriate and inappropriate cues, you lay the foundation to bypass this kind of downward spiral. And you're able to be world-class when it's time to shine.

 ZONED IN Acceleration Exercise:

Is there an upcoming situation where you will likely need to be highly agile and adjust? What are the empirical facts, and what is your possible interpretations for this event?

_____

_____

_____

_____

_____

How to Avoid Choking, Especially When It Matters

The Golden State Warriors, a champion U.S. NBA team, was favored to win the 2016 NBA finals, and extremely capable of doing so. They had the right players, a legendary coach, and they'd put in the hard work. Coming off a win the previous year, they were primed and ready to do it again.

It all came down to Game 7 at home, but the fairytale ending was not to be.

The Warriors were up against a force that couldn't be reckoned with, a team flanked by a giant whose physical presence and mental sharpness was impossible to penetrate, the Cleveland Cavaliers and LeBron James. The Cavaliers staved off elimination twice to force Game 7. The result? The Warriors lost, and the Cleveland Cavaliers won their first NBA title in franchise history.

James and his teammates were laser focused on one thing: doing whatever it took to win, every minute of the series. According to Richard Jefferson, a fellow Cavalier, James told the state of Ohio, "Get on my back, I got you. Get on my back and I'm going to carry you. I don't care if we fail, I'm going to wake up the next morning and I'm going to start working out and prepare for the next year."

As for the Warriors, did they choke? They certainly didn't play to their true potential throughout the series. Based on talent, team cohesion, and statistics, the Warriors should have won the NBA finals that year. Have you ever lost something that you could and should have won? I have, and it was no less important or painful to me than Game 7 for the Warriors. We are all susceptible to losing focus, making errors, and being unable to recover, especially in high pressure or high stakes situations.

What are the warning signs, and how can we recalibrate to finish as strong as possible? How can we get primed and ready when we don't have home court advantage, like the Cavaliers in Game 7? How can we be as agile as possible and avoid choking?

There are many important lessons to take from this example, and we can apply these to our own lives to avoid choking—especially when the stakes are high. Here are a couple ways to do that.

1. Detach yourself from the outcome

"I don't care if we fail," James said. Let me be very clear. Not caring about failing does *not* mean not caring about the outcome. Of course LeBron cared! He likely cared very deeply, just like you care about your results. What it means is surrendering to the possibility of failing. Making peace with it, so we can be laser-focused on what we do have control over.

Ultimately, this gives us the best chance of achieving what we want and deserve, because our mind is no longer distracted by past mistakes or possible future consequences. We are primed to be ZONED IN and to focus on the most important actions within our control.

2. **Play outside yourself**

"I'm going to come back home because I promised them that I would do something." LeBron James promised the entire city of Cleveland and the state of Ohio that he would bring back a championship after the franchise's 46-year dry spell. Who will you play for? Who needs you to show up and next-level your efforts or your performance?

If we can shift and detach ourselves from the outcome—and play for someone or something other than ourselves, we can not only avoid choking, but maybe even achieve levels of performance that we didn't know were possible.

As for the Warriors, they undoubtedly felt the sting of a devastating loss, learned from it, put their heads down, and worked even harder for the next season, which is what it means to be resilient. An unimaginable loss in Game 7 was their springboard to emerge once again as champions the following year. Defeat was their fuel, and they were 100% focused and primed for victory that next year.

ZONED IN Acceleration Exercise:

Think of an upcoming conversation, competition, performance, presentation, or situation where it's important for you to do well. What is the most important thing you have control over to do your best?

_____

_____

_____

_____

_____

Use Your RAS to Take Control of What You Want

When it comes to negative or positive events, fortunately we have a choice over what we focus on. At the base of your brain, where it connects with the spinal cord, your *reticular activating system (RAS)* subconsciously filters millions of bits of information that are flowing through your brain. Ruben Gonzalez, author of *The Courage to Succeed*, explains that your RAS is a bit like a computer's search engine. It only lets through the messages that you perceive as important. When they're given the green light, these thoughts are allowed into the cerebrum, where they are converted to conscious thoughts, emotions, or both.[18]

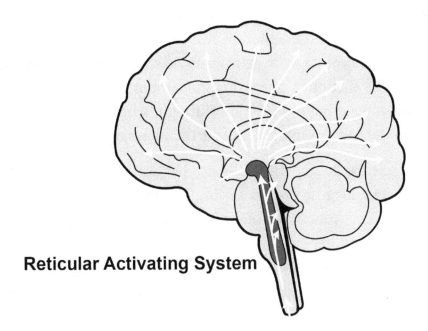

Reticular Activating System

Have you ever made the decision to buy a certain model, make, and color for your new car? And suddenly, that particular car seems to be everywhere? That's your RAS at work. You've told your RAS that this car is important to you. Another example is snapping out of a conversation in a busy room when you hear your name. You've learned over your lifetime that your name is important. How many times did your parents or teachers call your name growing up, especially when you were in trouble or danger? What about your spouse, partner, or friends over the years?

If you're a parent, how many times have you turned your head when you heard 'MOM!' or 'DAD!' and it ended up being someone else's child? You get the idea. This happens with whatever we consistently tell ourselves is important through repetition and the emotion we surround these thoughts with—it becomes important to us. As such, we need to tell our RAS that our biggest dream is important to us too, so it filters supporting information through, whether our dream is to be the best parent, athlete, partner, boss or friend.

The science behind this tells us that we have the power to bring our biggest dreams to life, but we must first see it to become it.[19] Your RAS seeks information that supports your beliefs, and filters the world through the guidelines you give it, which are your beliefs. If we don't believe our dream is possible at first, then we may have to act the part before we make it a reality. It's vital that we see ourselves as we want to be, rather than getting stuck in our current circumstances. Eventually, if we choose our thoughts wisely and are consistent, we'll believe that what we desire is possible and make it more likely to do what it takes to get there.

In order to do this, "I want ..." must become "I am ..." and "I want to contribute at a higher level and feel recognized and appreciated." becomes "I am a high-level contributor, and I am recognized and appreciated in my role." Likewise, "I want greater clarity and confidence in my life, so I can make my next big move" becomes "I am crystal clear on what I want, and I am confident in my ability to make my next big move." Once we start thinking this way, we are likely to start creating the actions to support our thoughts.

When we believe our dream is possible, shift our focus to live into that dream, and believe we are capable and deserving, our RAS champions our results and helps us get closer to the finish line. Why? Because we make a conscious effort to raise the importance of our next level of ambition, and we can believe achieving it is possible. Our vision then goes from narrow: "I can't" or "This is not possible" to broad: "I absolutely can" or "What else must I try?" "In other words, we go from not recognizing opportunities or the necessary next steps to being highly aware of these things. We go from not asking for help to searching out people or resources who can help us.

 ZONED IN Acceleration Exercise:

What is one control statement you can use to direct your RAS towards achieving what's most important to you now? How will you make it a habit to say it to yourself? And when? For example, "Every night when I brush my teeth, I'll say 'I am clear on what I want, and I am confident in my ability to succeed.'"

_____

_____

_____

_____

How to use your RAS, and how not use it

Most people are on autopilot and leave their RAS to chance to determine what's important and what isn't. But doing so can leave you open to discounting what's important to your success and imprinting what can hold you back. For example, you have a meeting with your manager where she praises you for the project you led and suggests a few improvements that would help you get the promotion you want. What do you signal as important or not important to your RAS? Hint: It should not be that your project was less than perfect.

The random thoughts we have will get us random results, so it's time to get in the driver's seat and tell our RAS what's important. That way, we start being more optimistic and more aware of opportunities to improve. What if we choose to tell ourselves repeatedly how amazing and important the praise is? 1) The things you did in your presentation register as important and memorable, so you're more likely to repeat them. 2) You're more likely to believe you're a good project leader and focus on making the necessary improvements to reach your desired result.

What you choose to consistently tell yourself is the driver for your success. If you believe you're a good project leader and capable of getting the promotion you want, you're more likely do what it takes consistently to achieve it.

But what happens if you consistently focus on things that are discouraging, negative, and hopeless? Since your RAS is a filter that only allows what's important into your conscious thought and looks for information to validate your beliefs, the likelihood of achieving your desired result is slim. When we consistently believe that our dreams/our goals are hopelessly unattainable, our efforts slow down or come to a complete halt. It's like a slow leak in a balloon that will eventually run out of air.

Essentially, our RAS helps us focus on what we tell it to see, which in turn influences our actions. It's time to choose whether you focus on the bad things, the limitations you place on yourself, and negativity, or focus on the possibilities that exist for you. By choosing to consistently focus on the latter, your RAS will be your ally, influencing how you see the world and therefore attracting what you need to succeed.

So, how can we maintain focus on progress and be resilient the next time we suffer an early exit, when others say we are not in shape, or when we lose? We can choose to put our RAS to work in a way that will help us keep moving forward. We can tell it our future ambitions are important and accessible.

ZONED IN Acceleration Exercise:

What regular thought do you have that you can consistently change from negative or discouraging to positive and optimistic every day? For example, "I am a perfectionist and get frustrated easily" to "I am in the process of recognizing my wins large and small."

_____

_____

_____

_____

_____

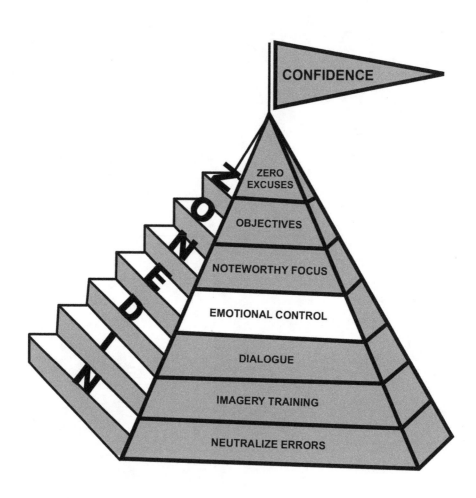

Chapter 5

EMOTIONAL CONTROL

The Key to Performing
When It Matters Most

"A quiet mind is able to hear intuition over fear." – Unknown

The ability to control our emotions during practice and competition is a powerful tool that world-class athletes have, and
that we can learn. Not being able to regulate emotions when
you're climbing is like putting a pie in the oven and leaving
the temperature to chance. You won't know what you're going
to get: under-done, just right, or burnt to a crisp. This chapter
will help you become world-class at raising your emotional
awareness, then using your emotions to your advantage.

Emotions and Their Lasting Effect

Four years and 3,600+ hours preparing consistently and diligently—and the day finally came. It was a perfect day in Santa Barbara, California: sunny, not too warm, and a light breeze. I had a great shot at winning the class, which was exciting considering how many years it took me to get to that point and how inexperienced my teammate (my horse) was. As I was at that time on deck waiting at the gate to enter the arena, the horse and rider before me maneuvered the course of 12 fences, clearing each one with ease. I thought about the sacrifice my parents had made for me, so I could compete in my sport. I also thought about what my trainer had told me the week before: to raise awareness about the privilege to participate in equestrian show-jumping.

"Riding is a sport of kings," she said. A sport that was not forgiving to a middle-class family's budget, I thought. My mind wandered back to past failures, when the unthinkable happened—I went off course resulting in a disqualification. Then I traveled forward, asking myself a question that evoked an increased heart rate, shallow breathing, and sweaty palms: "What if it happens again?" My mind was everywhere but where it should be, in the present moment. The gate to the arena opened. My name and number was called, and I was jolted from my fear of past failures and future what if's. But by then, my mind was everywhere except where it needed to be.

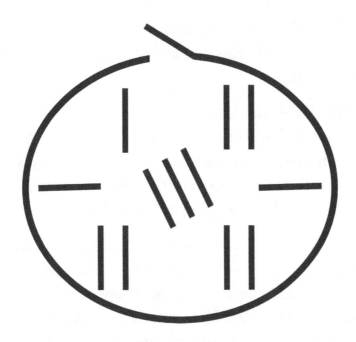

After the traditional respectful nod to acknowledge the judge of the competition, I began a roughly two-and-a-half-minute journey around twelve fences. I then caught sight of an opponent who had already had a near flawless round. My mind shifted from the present connection with my horse to the future. "What if I can't measure up?"

Fence one and two went well, then I looked for fence three, but didn't see it. Which one was it? In a split second, I was lost in the arena, impulsively making a left turn to what I thought was fence three, then knowing it wasn't.

My biggest fear materialized and robbed me of the best performance possible—and created the look of heartbreak on my parents' faces that I so desperately wanted to avoid. Four years and 3600+ hours of deliberate and focused practice for nothing, or so it felt.

From that day forward, fear of failure tempted me and won over and over. This fear was loyal, as it lingered like an unwanted admirer, throughout the remainder of my younger years and well into my first career. I thought: "Why put in all the hard work if I'm just going to fail again?"

Indeed, vivid and visceral negative emotions, such as a major disappointment or failure, can have a profound impact on memory and behavior as opposed to everyday occurrences. The more emotion, the stickier an event can become. And the more we are likely to imprint or remember what happened.[20] Fortunately, we can buck the system by learning how to manage and use emotions to our advantage. So, when the gate opens, you'll know how to show up and perform like a champion.

Are any past experiences affecting your current or future success? Any previous relationships or limiting beliefs standing between where you are and where you want to go? If so, it's time to face them, learn from them, and use them to reach your next level of ambition. If not, maybe it's time to dream even bigger and push towards a peak you may have thought was unattainable.

ZONED IN Acceleration Exercise:

Explain any past events, interactions, or experiences that may be affecting your current or future success. If you don't feel you have any, what's holding you back from going bigger or better?

_____

_____

_____

_____

_____

Similarities and Differences Between World-Class Performers and Everyone Else

Most of us experience the emotions associated with failure and setbacks, and most of us are susceptible to the emotional aftermath that arises from them. Consider this: fear, doubt, and frustration are just a few of the powerful emotions that do not discriminate between world-class performers and everyone else.

Negative emotions aren't reserved for the inexperienced or the not-famous. They are human emotions that have the power to elevate us to a level of success and joy we never thought possible—or disable our dream and turn it into a disappointing memory. There is a tremendous amount of hope if you want to next-level your ambitions, regardless of your past successes or failures.

Do world-class athletes and business professionals ever feel fear, doubt, frustration, and other negative emotions? You bet they do! In my experience of working with high school, college, and world-class athletes and senior leaders in Fortune 500 companies—negative emotions do not discriminate. The number one high school athlete moves on to play in Division 1, or the college player gets drafted to go pro. A Senior Vice President gets promoted to CEO, or a CEO must report poor earnings to investors.

Perhaps we all share emotions that don't serve our best performance and progress; however, there are a few key factors that separate world-class performers from everyone else. Having the toolset to be highly aware of our emotions—specifically which ones are constructive and which are destructive—then understanding how to use them to our advantage is where progress, courage, and success live. World-class performers do this remarkably well, and so can you.

Learning how to master your emotions and harness them requires you to think, practice, and compete in a different way. The result? A cheerleader, a coach, and a teammate you never knew you had—yourself. To access this new tool, you must first raise your current awareness level of your emotions. Then you must understand how world-class performers use these same emotions, positive and negative, to fuel their success.

An extreme example of this can be seen in the world of tennis, making an entertaining yet painful reminder of how our emotions can derail our performance.

It's difficult to argue what a great tennis player John McEnroe was, but his emotions hindered his chances at long-term success. 'In 1984 for example, when he beat Jimmy Connors at Wimbledon, it was a nearly perfect match for McEnroe-- with only three unforced errors, 78% of his first serves going in, and ten of them being aces.[25]

He even went on to win 78 of his 80 matches that year, which was astounding. In fact, George Plimpton once wrote that McEnroe was "the only player in the history of the game to go berserk and play better tennis." However, if he did crack the code and master how to use negative emotions to his advantage, it wasn't for long. Unfortunately, it was not sustainable. McEnroe was on a quest for perfection, and sport psychologists are very clear about the risk involved in this type of thinking and competing. McEnroe's fall from greatness started when he was just 25 years old.

We may or may not be legendary, but our quest for what matters is no less epic. McEnroe was an anomaly in that he could play insanely well despite being an emotional wreck at times, although it was unfortunately short-lived compared to the careers of other tennis greats. For most of us, performing our best while losing control of our emotions isn't possible. Negative emotions such as anger, fear, doubt, and frustration are distracting in a best-case scenario. In a worst-case scenario, they change our physiology by raising our heart rate, giving us sweaty palms, and encouraging our cognitive processes to shift from highly evolved to primitive. In other words, our ability to react and make decisions can suffer.[21]

A better example of mastering emotions for a sustainable long-term career is Roger Federer, who is considered one of the best tennis players in the open era. He has been playing at the professional level for 20 plus years and counting. Federer's calm and focused demeanor is a much better recipe for sustainable success. Does he experience a range of negative emotions? Likely yes, but he is clearly a master of how use them for his long-term success. And you can be too.

 ZONED IN Acceleration Exercise:

What is an instance where you feel fear or doubt? And how might it be holding you back?

_____

_____

_____

_____

How Your Mind Is Like a Clock

Whether we have an important presentation, interview, pitch, or crucial conversation, our best performance starts with being aware of where we are on our internal emotional clock at any given point in time.

The Emotional Clock

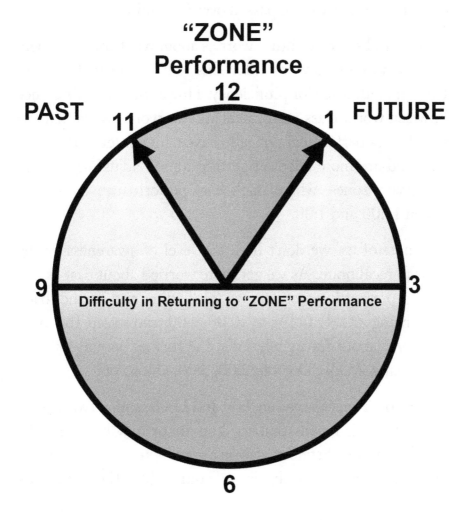

Let's say that being ZONED IN—an ideal frame of mind for competing or performing—is 12:00 o'clock. That's our performance homeostasis. Our ability to manage our emotions impacts whether we can arrive at or recover to 12:00 o'clock. If we start to worry about past poor performance during an important situation, we are in danger of slipping backwards from 12:00 to 11:00. For example, if we think back to when we missed consecutive shots in tennis, a presentation was not well-received, or we got passed over for a raise.

If our mind shifts to future worries about what could happen, we start to move toward 1:00. This is 100% normal and can happen at all levels of proficiency. However, a key difference between world-class performers and everyone else is that the world-class performers typically have a higher level of awareness and are more adept at getting to and adjusting back to the green zone—where one's best performance lives—between 11:00 and 1:00.

For most of us, we don't have the level of awareness or the tools to recalibrate. As we get more worried about past events during present interactions, we fall further and further back from being ZONED IN, to 10:00, 9:00, and so on. The more we worry about future what if's, the further we fall forward from being ZONED IN to 2:00, 3:00, and so on.

The yellow zone is between 9:00 and 11:00, and between 1:00 and 3:00. This means caution. You are or may be approaching an emotional state that won't serve you on your quest to practice or compete to the best of your ability. The good news is that with the proper tools, you can recover and get back to the green zone.

Unfortunately, there's bad news too. If you're unaware of your emotions, or you're aware but don't maintain the ability to adjust them, you can go from caution to danger. The red zone is a dangerous place to be in, because recovering back to 12:00 or being ZONED IN is nearly impossible without stepping out of the arena and taking the time to regroup.[22]

The red zone is likely where John McEnroe lived for much of his short but impressive career. Unfortunately, most of us don't have the ability to perform when we are berserk and our emotions are running wild. Plus, we want to perform over the long haul, right? Think of it this way, John McEnroe's emotions were spinning around the emotional wheel. The hands eventually flew off and the wheel broke. My wish is for you to perform your best over the long-term, to get and stay in the green, so you can achieve and sustain a level of success that you desire and deserve.

What if our emotions do get the best of us during an important situation and we find ourselves in the red zone? Since it's difficult, if not impossible, to recover on the fly or when you're in the moment, it's best to take a break to regain your composure. Say you're giving a presentation and you're getting challenged, so you feel threatened and overwhelmed. Your fear of failure is getting worse, and you sense that you're unable to get back on course. Your heart rate is increasing, your palms are sweating, and you're unable to focus on what's most important. It may be time to excuse yourself briefly, regain your composure, and start moving the needle back to the top of the clock.

In the next section, I'll show you how you can avoid the danger zone altogether.

 ## ZONED IN Acceleration Exercise:

List/name an upcoming event that could cause you to feel fearful, worried, or anxious. Then write one thing that may move you away from being ZONED IN or in your green zone.

_____

_____

_____

_____

Optimizing Your Emotions Using RRS

If you put in the deliberate work consistently, have enough talent, and are capable, you should win in the moments that matter, right? Not necessarily.

For me, it was performance-related anxiety that affected my ability to compete. The result? Frustration and disappointment to say the least. So I wanted to make sure this didn't happen to anyone else. I wanted to learn how, after consistent and deliberate practice, we could put our best foot forward in the moments that mattered most, like an Olympian who trained her whole life for her two minutes to shine.

There's a simple (but not always easy!) formula that I teach to world-class athletes and business people, and it can yield significant results for you too. It doesn't guarantee a W, but it will help you regulate your emotional clock to stay in the green zone in the moments that matter. It will also help you be happy and proud that you did your absolute best when the pressure was on. It's called the RRS Formula™.

1. **Recognize** an emotion that does not serve you. Often, we pass from green to yellow and even to red on the emotional wheel without being aware of what's happening until it's too late. So, step one is to raise your awareness level going into a high-pressure or high-stakes situation. Are you nervous, worried, calm, anxious ...?

2. **Release** an emotion that does not serve you. One way to do this is take 3-5 deep belly breaths in through your nose and out through your mouth, both for a slow count of 5. Listen to your breathing or imagine your favorite color when exhaling. These are effective ways of clearing your mind of past worries and future concerns that are out of your control. When done effectively, you can

return to the green zone to become ZONED IN. Be patient, because like anything else, this takes practice. I recommend trying the recognize and release phases in less important situations to start.

3. **Strategize** by deciding what's most important that you have control over in that moment, and then usher your thoughts there. One way to do this is to ask yourself the very question, "What is most important to my best performance that I have control over right now?" This is a way of you taking control of your performance and not allowing it to control you.

For example, the downhill skier who has practiced her whole life and is in the chute waiting for the bull horn may *recognize*: "I'm worried that I'll need to be ultra-fast to get on to the podium." She *releases*, taking three deep breaths, inhaling through her nose, feeling her stomach extend, then breathing out through her mouth—laser focused on the sound that her breath makes when the warm air exits her mouth. Now, back in the green zone, she strategizes to herself, "Stay low, skis together."

Whether you're at work or at home, you may compete for your own personal Olympics often. If you remember this formula using the acronym RRS and practice it regularly, you'll be able to better regulate your emotions, so you can be happy and proud of the moments you work hard for.

ZONED IN Acceleration Exercise:

For the upcoming event that could make you feel fearful, worried, or anxious, write how you could:

1. Recognize: _____

2. Release: _____

3. Strategize: _____

_____

_____

_____

_____

A Secret about "the F Word"

Is it possible that sometimes, simply "releasing" doesn't work? Absolutely. Maybe you're so fearful that a couple of deep belly breaths aren't going to move the needle from yellow back to green. It's important to understand that fear has an important place in accelerating progress and performing your best, especially under pressure. It just depends on which lens you view fear through, and how you're equipped to use it. The good news is there's a technique that can help you turn fear into your biggest ally, though it may seem against human nature to most. Rather than fear enticing you into the red zone and leaving you there, paralyzed and unable to recover to your best performance—you can use it to your advantage.

Think for a moment how David beat Goliath. Was he bigger, stronger, or better equipped? Absolutely not. Was David afraid of his own demise? Very likely. There's one thing David did when he volunteered or more accurately *demanded* to go head to head with Goliath on the front line of battle. What David did can make all the difference the next time you're confronted with fear. He surrendered to his fear, learned from it and then decided to proceed strategically anyway.

Most of us try to push fear away and encourage others to do the same. "Don't worry, it will be fine," we tell ourselves, our friends, colleagues, and our kids. But from both an evolutionary and current standpoint, this reasoning is flawed. We have a built-in biological fight or flight response to protect ourselves from danger. When triggered, our heart rate and blood pressure increase, our pupils dilate to let in more light, our muscles tense up energized by adrenaline and glucose, and we have trouble focusing on small tasks, so we can focus on the one most important thing: fighting or fleeing a potentially dangerous situation.

Suppressing this biological response can have serious consequences. When we were hunters and gatherers thousands of years ago, this faulty logic could get us killed. We'd sense the danger of a saber-toothed tiger lurking around the corner, convince ourselves that "It will be fine," then get eaten. Now, we're not likely to get eaten by a tiger or die if a pitch, presentation, or crucial conversation doesn't go well, but fear still provides us with important information that we must bring closer to us—rather than push away.

In Gavin de Becker's novel *Gift of Fear*, he explains that our gut feelings are no joke when it comes to protecting us from potentially dangerous situations. As a matter of fact, your next gut feeling could save your life, says de Becker. The basic idea is that sometimes we take in information quicker than we can cognitively process it. Whether your gut is giving you life- or career-saving information, it should not be discounted.

The next time you experience a gut feeling and it makes you fearful, it's there for you to pay attention to—not to push away. An important competition, meeting, conversation, or interview is not a matter of life or death, but in those situations, it is important to court the fear, learn from it, and not be afraid of it. If you sense fear, it may be for a good reason. Even if there is a lot riding on what you're about to do, your reactions must be brought forward—from the time of hunter gatherers 10,000 years ago to the present day.

David's gut likely told him he could die, which rightfully could make him fearful. But rather than step back from fear, he brought it closer and learned from it. "If I don't want to get defeated by Goliath, what must I do?" As the story goes, Goliath had poor sight due to a physical abnormality, and the only spots not protected by armor were between his eyes. So David used a slingshot to launch a stone right between Goliath's eyes to disable him. David learned from his fear and used it as a superpower.

Sometimes, we must be David. We must look fear in the face, motion it towards us, and ask it to whisper what's so important that we need to know. When we know, we can view fear as our biggest ally or cheerleader, standing next to us yelling "YOU KNOW WHAT TO DO. I TOLD YOU. NOW GO!"

The next time you're called upon to battle, compete, present, or speak up, how will you listen and learn from your gut? How will you fight for what is rightfully yours? Will you retreat where it feels safe, or will you look fear in the face and listen to what it has to say?

We can face our fear

I believe in you, and I believe that you are capable of succeeding beyond fear and beyond your current circumstances. I've seen the transformation in hundreds of clients once they learn how to be mentally tough and how to not just confront fear but use it to their advantage.

Personally, I was fearful for over 20 years. Fearful that no one would understand the importance of mental toughness. That no one would be receptive to what I had to say. That I wasn't smart enough to build a successful business out of what I was passionate about. Who was I to inspire others to greatness if I had not achieved greatness on a grand scale myself?

Here's what changed:

1. I realized I had achieved greatness. I consistently helped my private practice clients one by one to see a transformation and a level of joy that they never thought possible. I raised three intelligent, compassionate, and giving children who make me a better person.

2. I decided it was time for my business to scale to help many instead of a few, and I granted myself permission to do so.

I decided it was time to listen to my gut and carry on the legacy of my father who said "Sheryl, if you are resilient, focused, and consistent, you can achieve anything." I didn't know how to be resilient and recover from failure when I first heard those words over four decades ago, or how to focus in the moments when we must be our most courageous selves.

But I do now, and you can learn too.

ZONED IN Acceleration Exercise:

Write down/list one important task or event that you've been putting off that scares you. How will you listen to your gut, look fear in the face, and commit to the action you already know to take? Who is depending on you to do this?

_____

_____

_____

_____

_____

Understanding Emotions, Memory, and Performance

In 1989, during my first career, I worked in San Francisco at a well-known investment banking firm. I normally arrived home in the East Bay by 4:00 p.m. On October 17, I stayed in the city to get a haircut. On my way to the bus, I felt the sidewalk move a little. Living in California my whole life, it was no big deal. Just a little earthquake.

Then, at 5:04 p.m., everything and everyone fell quiet. The clocks on the buildings stopped, the taxis came to a halt, and the normal sounds of a busy city were now silent. We'd just experienced a 6.9 earthquake. I couldn't get home because the Bay Bridge, which connects the East Bay and San Francisco, had suffered major damage. The BART train was deemed unsafe, and there were no trains running until further notice. There was no way home, and I was scared.

I remember looking at the clock on one of the buildings where the black hands were frozen at 5:04 p.m., glancing down at the light grey dress slacks I was wearing, and the number on the first cab I tried to hail when I realized the seriousness of the situation. Those three things are still vivid in my memory today.

Emotions are what cement experiences like these throughout our lives. Unfortunately, the memories we'd rather forget can have more intensity than the pleasant ones. However, there is a way to control our emotions to minimize the effect of negative experiences and use these emotions to our advantage, rather than to our detriment.

What are the consequences if you don't control your emotions? If you allow negative emotions to run wild with no system to manage and harness their power? Best-case scenario, negative emotions are distracting. More likely, they will rob you of your motivation, progress, and desire to do what it takes to cross the finish line. When negativity and pessimism are your default, especially when challenges arise, it can make small obstacles seem unsurmountable.[23]

Here are a few ways you can use your emotions to create more *productive* memories to fuel your success:

1. **Create strong positive emotions after an event:**

    When you do something well, it's important to be highly aware and attach a lot of emotion to it. Say in an important sales meeting, you engage with your prospect in a powerful way. Or during a presentation, you command the room and feel confident. During or as soon as possible after the event, it's helpful to recognize what you did and how it felt—and make it as detailed and visceral as possible. Don't just wait for the big wins! The small wins are important too.

    Also, be sure to celebrate the process rather than just the outcome. Let's say in the sales meeting, you had high energy, acknowledged your prospect's struggle, and offered a solution that your prospect hadn't thought of. Then, you challenged her to make the best decision. No convincing and no real selling required. Deal closed. But deal closed or not, it's appropriate and necessary to celebrate the successful sales process. You might think, "Yes, high energy, acknowledge, solution, challenge!"

⭐ *ZONED IN Acceleration Exercise:*

What is one way you can create a strong positive emotion for an important upcoming event?

_____

_____

_____

_____

2. **Details, details, details:**

So, you know that it's easier to remember events when we surround our wins with a lot of emotion. Let's go a step further by adding details to the charged statement "Yes! high energy, acknowledge, solution, challenge!" and attach specific details to each step. Take control over what you choose to imprint, and make it as detailed as possible.

- For **energy**, on a scale of one to ten, what level of energy did you bring to the conversation? What were your tone, eye contact, presence, posture, use of hands/arms, etc.?

- For **acknowledge**, what did you say to let your prospect know you heard their problem/challenge? How did you let them know you cared?

- For **solution**, what made our recommendation really resonate?

- For **challenge**, what question did you ask to get the prospect to understand your solution? For example, "Based on your sense of urgency, desired outcome of a, b, and c, I imagine your choice will be an easy one?"

 ZONED IN Acceleration Exercise:

What are three details of an upcoming event in your direct control, which are most important to your success (for example, delivering a presentation with confidence, energy, and precision)?

_____

_____

_____

_____

3. **Increased emotional arousal is more important than the information:**

Has your child (or someone else's) ever been so excited about an ice cream cone, a new puppy, or the newest gadget that you bought it even though it was against your better judgment? Conversely, when you were in an important meeting or conversation where the speaker was very monotone, how did you respond to their words? With excitement and willingness to take action or with only your partial attention?

Even if what you say is 100% correct, important to the other person, or potentially impactful, it's in danger of falling on deaf ears or not having the impact it could— if you don't attach a high level of emotion to it. In other words, how we make people feel can be even more important than what we say.[24]

Expressing emotion in our own thoughts—the conversations we have with ourselves—is important too. When we do this effectively, we are better able to commit a task to subconscious memory, freeing up mental space for something new. In order to do this though, we must attach emotion to the process of improving as well as the small and large victories we experience. For example, a sprinter might listen to an upbeat playlist while practicing her starts, and then include a fist pump at the end of an exceptionally good one.

Conversely, there is a different type of emotion surrounding defeat, setbacks, negative emotion. You can now understand how detrimental to performance this can be, but unfortunately it can be a common default. Imagine if you could learn to generate a similar level of emotion that you experience during your biggest failure or embarrassment, then channel it to what you're trying to improve upon. You absolutely can, but it starts with how you communicate with yourself, and how you interpret what's important.

Our internal dialogue, especially what we hear over and over, is our truth—what we believe. It can be our biggest motivator and source of encouragement, or it can have the power to defeat us. The combination of emotions and our internal dialogue is powerful and, when used properly, can help accelerate progress towards our next big win. You'll learn how in the next chapter.

 ## ZONED IN Acceleration Exercise:

What is one way you can you can use a negative emotion and channel it to better serve you? For example, if you're practicing for that presentation and you're worried about the outcome, shift the worry to eye contact during it and the emotions you'll feel when receiving a standing ovation.

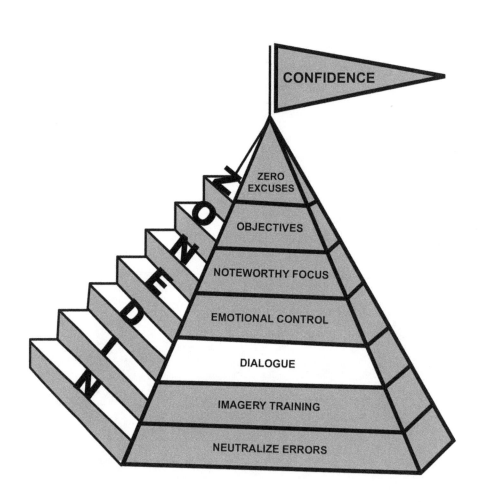

Chapter 6

DIALOGUE

How to Have a Voice of Success

"If you think you can do a thing, or you think you can't do a thing, you're right." – Henry Ford

There are a few things that create a gap between world-class performers and everyone else. It's not that they're all necessarily geniuses, well-connected, better looking, more talented, or any other genetic or innate reason you may think of. On the contrary, it's been proven that ordinary people *can* become extraordinary thanks to three plus decades of impactful research and science.

So, what sets the achievers apart from the dreamers, and how can we use this science to persevere, be resilient, and be able to perform our best in those important moments? In this chapter, you'll discover a tool that sets the world-class performers apart and gives them the mental toughness required to keep going. We'll also look at the importance of celebrating triumphs large *and* small, and why a world-class dialogue is vital to your personal success. Finally, we'll discuss how to make the dialogue shift from novice to pro.

Bridging the Gap

On one side of the personal success chasm are those who have a vision larger than themselves and believe that what they yearn for is possible, even in the face of nay-sayers, defeat, or setbacks. These are the resilient optimists, who are courageous and confident on their steady march to victory. Those who are quick to dust themselves off and get back in the arena. Those who are quick to ask for help. And those who proceed as if success is inevitable.

On the other side are those who may have a vision for what they yearn for, but in their heart, they don't believe it's possible. Perhaps the most fatal difference is how they *explain defeat* to themselves, in a way that's pessimistic, permanent ("I will never achieve this"), and pervasive ("I'm not only incapable at the task at hand, I am incapable in other areas of my life too"). Doing so has been proven to be an unsurmountable barrier to success.[25]

So, how do we close the gap and leap to the side where personal success and joy live? How can we execute what science has proven we *can* achieve?

Our personal success starts with the dialogue we have with ourselves every day. Those intimate, consistent, and influential thoughts that—if repeated enough—we believe as the truth. These repeated conversations determine our reality, and they influence our actions.[26]

As discussed in the previous chapter, the more emotion we attach to a conversation, either positive or negative, the more likely it will be committed to our memory. When it comes to large triumphs such as getting married or receiving a sizable promotion, you may react with lots of positive emotion, which is a signal that it's important to you. Conversely, a lesser triumph such as making it to the gym after a three-week hiatus may not be recognized or celebrated as much, and therefore not register as important.

First, consider that your internal voice is shaped by many different factors. The most significant may be your parents or other influential people in your life, as well as past experiences. It's time to choose which thoughts we keep with us and which things we tell ourselves are important.

Is your first time back to the gym important to your long-term well-being? Yes! So, use your inner voice to tell yourself that it's important. If you do, you may be more likely to continue down the path of making the wellness routine a habit.[27] Be consistent in telling yourself what's possible in the long term and what's important for you to accomplish today.

It's time to say to yourself (in the present tense): "I am in the process of becoming healthy and fit, and today I work out vigorously for 30 minutes." Or "I achieve senior leader status, and today I present with confidence and authority." Step ahead of your current circumstances and start *conversing with yourself* as if you are already the person you want to become. Those baby steps are a big deal and can add up to a big win, so use your internal voice consistently to believe and to drive your progress.

 ZONED IN Acceleration Exercise:

What is one way that you can shift a previously negative dialog towards a more resilient, optimistic dialog?

_____

_____

_____

_____

The Tone of Your Success

Growing up, we were taught how to speak to our parents, grandparents, teachers, siblings, and peers. From a young age, we were expected to be respectful, encouraging, and at a minimum, civil. When we fell short, maybe we heard "Do not speak to me in that tone young man/lady!" Maybe we have given the same warning to our kids, possibly when a child or teen was trying to exercise their independence.

It's safe to say that there's a societal norm regarding what constitutes an appropriate tone for subordinates, peers, and superiors in both social and work contexts. There are also volumes of research and advice on the importance of tone in personal and work relationships, and in leadership styles.

Tone matters in crucial conversations, possibly even more than the words themselves.[28] It's our tone that can encourage others to help us, hear us out, or be receptive. It's also our tone that can make others discouraged, closed off, and upset. Even words such as "I love you" can get the most well-intentioned person into surprisingly hot water when they're said in a dejected and negative tone.

Unfortunately, we get far less guidance growing up (if any) on the tone we take with ourselves. Did we learn from our parents what tone to take with ourselves when we fail or become frustrated? In my experience, not typically. Similar to the backlash we get from others when our tone is condescending, mean, curt, or negative, the consequences of not understanding how to have a respectful, encouraging, and baseline civil tone with ourselves can be significant roadblocks to our personal success.

The tone of our internal voice after we fail or misstep tends to descend and get deeper. Our inflections on what we interpret as bad are more pronounced. For example, a client named Susan explained what happened after an unsuccessful interview for a senior marketing position. She said, "It was *terrible*," and pronounced *terrible* in a much deeper tone (descending) with a much higher level of emphasis (inflection) than the first two words. When we stress key words, especially negative ones, we signal to ourselves and others that this word is important. To make matters even worse, sometimes we draw out the word (such as *t-e-r-r-i-b-l-e*) and put even more importance on the very thing that is causing us anguish.

When a negative and judgmental tone is our default ("I'm terrible at interviews and will never get promoted"), then we're more likely to think of our failure as permanent, and therefore not fixable. That's not conducive to progress and resilience. Rather than seek out ways to improve for next time, we'll be more frustrated and not likely to take the required action to learn and improve, so we can nail the next interview, pitch, conversation, etc.

The next time you experience a setback, misstep, or failure, there are a few things you can do to develop a world-class tone.

First, have a *curious* tone rather than a judgmental one. It's okay to acknowledge what happened and how you feel, but be curious about *why* it happened, rather than being hard on yourself.

For example, "My interview didn't go well, and that's frustrating ... I'm curious whether it was anything I said or did, or whether I'm not right for this job? How can I **improve** for my next interview?" Place the inflection on *improve*. This curious tone isolates the bad interview to a singular event: "this job". The calm tone removes the importance of the bad interview and how frustrating it was. The inflection on "improve" is a signal that improving is important, making it more likely that you'll seek out ways to do so. Essentially, having a curious tone when we stumble is a way to encourage ourselves to dust off and get back into arena, increasing our ability to be as agile as possible.

Second, have an *empathetic* and *encouraging* tone. Think about how you treat a friend or family member when they come up short. What would you say to them, and in what tone? We tend to be our own worst critics, which is not conducive to getting what we want and deserve. But we need to step into the cheerleader and coach role if we want to emerge as champions.

Bottom line: it's not just what we say to ourselves, but the tone we say it in. If we tend to devalue the good with a neutral tone (when you make a small sale, you say it's "pretty good" or "okay"), then sensationalize the not-so-good (when you are rejected by a prospect and tell yourself "I am TERRIBLE at selling"), our desired result may be challenging at best. It's like a small snowball that becomes giant and life-threatening. We've taken an experience that we want to scale and not registered it as important. Then we over-emphasize an action that *we do not* want to repeat.

Tone is a powerful tool that helps world-class performers instruct their thoughts, emotions, and actions to fuel their success. It's time to place greater value on the good by amplifying your tone for the successes you have, no matter how big or small.

 ZONED IN Acceleration Exercise:

Write about a past event that was not ideal. What was your tone with yourself, and how did it affect your progress? Then write how you can shift your tone, so you can recover and make progress next time.

_____

_____

_____

_____

_____

Affirmations: How to Create a Voice2Win

Katherine was a brilliant and well-recognized human resources director in her industry two decades ago. After a long hiatus from work to raise a family, she was ready to re-enter the workforce. She not only wanted to go back to work, but she *had to* support herself and her family. Katherine was incredibly driven and highly capable, but increasingly frustrated because she wasn't seeing the results she desired. She wasn't getting called back consistently in the interview process.

Over and over, this is what she said: "Who will hire me since I have no recent experience? What if I put in all the effort of organizing my resume and interviewing, then it's all for nothing? I really dropped the ball for not staying involved in my industry somehow over the years."

Katherine was so consistent with these negative, recurring thoughts that she believed them as truth. In her mind, she *was* unqualified, undeserving, and incapable of being hired, so why put in the work to bring her resume and experience up to date? She didn't believe that what she wanted was possible, which in turn disabled her motivation and progress. No consistent connecting on LinkedIn, no networking events, no reaching out to past colleagues. Nada. *What's the point?* She convinced herself.

So, how do we focus on progress rather than perfection, and turn a judgmental and critical voice into one that propels us forward, rather than one that drags us down? Well, we can start by using our internal voice to practice daily affirmations.

While affirmations can help us to achieve specific goals, they can also do much more according to the Chopra Institute, which was founded in 1996 by Deepak Chopra, M.D. and David Simon, M.D., to provide an integrative approach to total well-being through self-awareness, and the practice of yoga, meditation, and Ayurveda. Affirmations are meant to "encourage a life filled with positivity and gratitude."[29] Once we achieve our goal, we can replace the affirmation with another one. This encourages a level of success and joy in the achievement, rather than discounting our progress and moving on to the next desired result, leaving us unfulfilled and not as happy. Evidence-based research shows that affirmations change the brain on a cellular level. In other words, what you think about and how you talk to yourself matters—a lot.[30]

"Thoughts have a direct connection to your emotional and physical health," says Dr. Joseph Dispenza, author of *Physics, the Brain and Your Reality*. As such, it's important to be aware of your affirmations and choose them wisely. Skeptical? Here's a little science to explain. Positive self-affirmations activate reward centers in the brain, which are the same areas that respond to good experiences such as eating your favorite ice cream or receiving a complement.[31]

This is significant, because it's these areas that help us lessen pain, such as defeat or failure, and help us maintain our composure during perceived threats, such as in an important interview or presentation. In Katherine's case, these parts of her brain weren't being activated, allowing defeat and her perceived threats to disrupt her progress.

Here are some ways you can use affirmations to create a winning voice:

1. **Develop a can-do attitude:** Remember, sometimes,
   we must be actors or actresses to create this voice of
   success. Maybe it's unlikely that a goal will happen, or
   uncertain whether you'll perform at the level you hope
   for. Even so, it's important to believe you can reach
   your biggest dream or achieve rock star status when it
   really matters, and affirming this over and over is part
   of this process. Affirmations can help you do this, as
   Harvard psychologist and TED speaker Amy Cuddy
   says, "Fake it until you become it."

2. **Stay positive:** When positive affirmations are repeated
   ("I am smart enough to reach my biggest dream" or "I
   am active and lean"), they do more than just make you
   feel good. They help you believe you *are* good, which
   raises your self-efficacy. This can be a huge motivator
   and cheerleader, especially when it gets difficult or you
   suffer a setback.

3. **Check out ThinkUp™:** I've had the honor of working
   with Irit Wald, CEO and Founder of the positive affirmations app ThinkUp™ (http://thinkup.me). Essentially, it combines positive affirmations with your own
   voice and music to change not just the way you think,
   but also what you *do*. You can try it for free at www.
   sherylkline.com/thinkup. (Disclaimer: I am an affiliate
   of ThinkUp.)

Try creating and listening to these affirmations every night before bed for five minutes.

Keep in mind that it's very common for us to judge ourselves based on other people's sizzle reels, rather than what's real. We don't see the struggle and insecurities of other people. Rest assured, it's there at any level—whether you're an amateur athlete or an Olympian, an intern or the CEO, a new mother or the household CEO of four teens.

Everyone struggles at some point. It's a sisterhood and a brotherhood that does not discriminate in its membership, so please start thinking about the change or transformation you want to see in your life. A great way to start doing this is using positive affirmations. You have it within you to achieve what you yearn for, and it starts with using your internal voice to affirm that *you can.*

 ZONED IN Acceleration Exercise:

Complete the positive affirmations worksheet at https://www.sherylkline.com/p/positive-affirmations. Write about one positive affirmation you will begin repeating to yourself.

_____

_____

_____

_____

Your Instructional Voice

Have you ever had a coach or a manager give you direction on what's most important for the task at hand? For example, a tennis coach may say, "You're going to practice hitting balls down the line to get better at passing shots." A manager may announce an agenda for a team meeting, the desired outcomes, and why they're important. This sets an intention for the practice or meeting to keep the activity as focused and productive as possible. Without setting intentions, progress is left to randomness, which at best is inefficient.

What about how we use our voice to instruct ourselves when we're on task? How can we direct our thoughts to make our practice as impactful as possible, and therefore accelerate our progress?

Until about 10 years ago, it was generally believed that the answer was: we couldn't. In other words, it was common knowledge that human intention couldn't affect our physical reality.[32] For example, if you set an intention to be calm in a stressful situation, there would be no effect on your perceived stress level, and you would certainly not have the ability to affect your physical symptoms.

However, research now suggests that we absolutely *can* use our intentions to change our beliefs, our physical reality, and therefore influence what we achieve. In 2007, *The Intention Experiment* examined the science of intention, using research from Princeton, MIT, Stanford, and other universities to prove that intentions are very capable of affecting many different aspects of our lives.[33]

Here's an example I use: "Sheryl, it's time to take consistent action toward your goal of influencing 10,000 people to become mentally tough this year, so they can experience the joy of seeing a transformation they want and deserve." How can you use an instructional voice to direct your thoughts towards your next level of ambition?

"(Your name), it's time to take consistent action toward
_____, *so that* _____."

There's no right or wrong here. Just what's most important to you now—and a personal statement of instruction to take consistent action.

In the short term, an instructional voice directs attention to your most important controllable action, so you'll get laser-focused on the task at hand. For my one-on-one clients and group clients, it's common practice for them to set intentions whenever practicing or preparing to compete. To help get laser-focused on a task, a highly important conversation, competition, or presentation, consider using this instructional voice with yourself to prepare:

"(Your name), you are _____, *and right now it's most important for you to* _____. *Go."*

For example, if you're preparing for an important pitch at work, you might say:

"(Your name), you are capable of closing this deal, and it's most important for you to execute the sales process." This is under the assumption that the 'sales process' is mastered. If not, I'd get more detailed by focusing on the most important part of the process necessary to for the process to be a success.

Still not convinced? Dr. Richard Davidson is a professor of psychology and psychiatry at the University of Wisconsin-Madison, and founder of the Center of Healthy Minds. Dr. Davidson and his team's work focuses on neuroplasticity of the brain (our brain's ability to change and adapt) to induce positive change.

Through his and his team's research, we're learning that *"We can shape our brains in more adaptive and beneficial ways by cultivating healthy habits of mind...When given a challenging situation your brain hasn't encountered before, it can reorganize and restructure to respond to that situation. The more often your brain is exposed to that new challenge—like learning a musical instrument, for instance—the more it reorganizes and makes that path more established...Our brains are constantly being shaped wittingly or unwittingly—most of the time unwittingly."* [41]

Simply put, it's possible to change our neural connections by the way we instruct or talk to ourselves over and over. So, we need to become more aware of what these instructions are and make sure our instructional voice is positive, encouraging, and optimistic. If we continue unwittingly, the default—especially after failure or a setback—is unlikely to instruct us towards our best efforts in the short or long term.

Progress towards your personal success, however defined by you, can be a winding path. It can be very difficult, plagued with setbacks, failures, etc. As a result, it's important to consistently instruct yourself using your internal voice towards your desired result rather than allow setbacks, defeat, and failures to be unwelcome guests for too long.

Now you've achieved noteworthy focus and understand the principles of emotional control, you can use your instructional voice to direct your thoughts. This will allow you to move successfully into learning about imagery training, the small movies that will help champion your results.

ZONED IN Acceleration Exercise:

Write one instruction for yourself in an area where it's important for you to improve. When and how will you make a practice of incorporating this into your daily routine?

_____

_____

_____

_____

_____

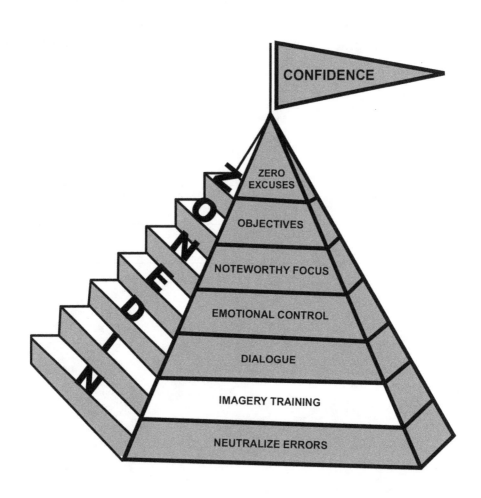

Chapter 7

IMAGERY TRAINING

Creating an Accelerated
Vision of Success

*"If you aren't engaged in a consistent mental imagery
program, you're not doing everything you can to achieve
your (athletic) goals." – Dr. Jim Taylor*

When Olympians compete, their venue, techniques, and victory are already familiar to them. U.S. Olympic swimmer Missy Franklin won four gold medals at the 2012 London Games, and as she described, "When I got there, I've already pictured what's going to happen a million times, so I don't actually have to think about it."[34]

At any given Olympic games, there is a team of sport psychologists to help athletes maximize their potential (for example, the United States Olympic Team provided eight for the 2016 Rio Games). One of their most important jobs is to guide athletes through a successful competition *before* it happens as well as helping them to practice their craft using their mind. The result is an accelerated progress and a greater level of calm and focus during competition.

But Olympians are not the only ones trying to achieve their best! We have the same 24 hours in a day and only so much time to practice our sport, presentation, pitch, or important conversation. How do *we* make progress faster, and how do we practice prior to arriving at the starting line? The advanced tool to help us with this is **imagery training**, and you can have it in your back pocket, so you can get better quicker.

The Power of Imagery Training

Kayla Harrison, a 26-year-old judoka (Judo athlete), is extremely detailed in her visualization exercises. Months and even years before the Rio Games arrived, she practiced imagery training for 10 minutes before falling asleep each night, mentally going through entire days of Olympic competition. "Waking up, weighing in, packing my bag, getting on the bus, listening to certain music," she said. "Every night I visualize myself winning the Olympics." She then went on to defend her Olympic judo title in Rio.[35]

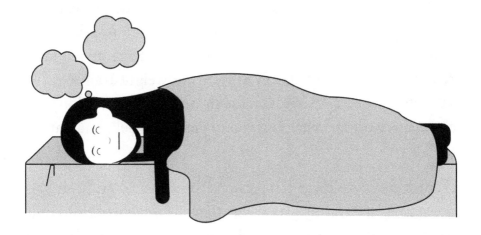

Not a world-class swimmer or an expert Judo athlete? No problem. The science says that imagery training can help anyone—not just Olympians.[36]

Amazingly, we can generate information from memory that is similar to an actual experience. In other words, the images we create in our mind can have the same effect on our nervous system as if we were executing the event in real time. The science of how it works is called *psychoneuromuscular theory.* Simply, when we have a thought, it generates small impulses in our brain and our muscles. The detail of these thoughts and small muscle movements depend on the detail of the instructions we give ourselves.

A study at of the University of Chicago asked basketball participants to only visualize and not physically practice shooting free throws for a month. They improved their actual shooting by 23%.[37] Amazingly, you can also put imagery training to work if you want to get stronger, even if you don't put in time at the gym. A study conducted by Guang Yue, an exercise physiologist at the Cleveland Clinic Foundation, asked volunteers to imagine flexing their biceps as hard as possible. After a few weeks of simply visualizing weight training, the subjects showed a 13.5% increase in strength![38] I wouldn't bet on imagery training helping you to get a six-pack, but you get the idea.

If a world-class athlete can produce the same electrical signals using imagery training as when they are practicing or competing, imagine what you might be able to accomplish if you use the same techniques to prepare for your next important event.

Here are a couple of instances where you could use imagery training to help your performance:

1. **Periodically during the day:** Whenever you have an important "competition" (a presentation, performance, or crucial conversation), or any time you must take action and might be feeling a little anxious or under pressure.

2. **Before bed and when you wake up:** If you include imagery training before going to sleep, these thoughts can carry over into your subconscious. If you do the same when you wake up, you can reinforce them.[39]

3. **During practice:** If you can positively structure an experience before practicing, it can help you get laser-focused prior to starting. You'll prime your mind and your muscles to give 100% when you practice, therefore accelerating progress. If you do this just after you practice by replaying what you've practiced, all the better.

In addition to training your brain for actual performance, it's been found that imagery training can affect motor control (or control of your muscles), attention, perception, planning, and memory. It can also enhance motivation and increase confidence and self-efficacy—your belief that you can accomplish a task.[40]

What does that mean for you? Imagery training not only helps you accelerate progress, but can help you future-cast your ambitions beyond your current circumstances. You'll believe in your capabilities and develop the confidence required to take consistent action. You'll *live into* the person you want to become in the future—today. This is because you're using imagery training to "see" that person every day and therefore manifest what it takes to step into those shoes.

Remember your reticular activating system (RAS)? Imagery training is a way of consistently controlling and filtering the highly important information through. You take control and put what you desire in the forefront of your mind. By doing so, you are highly aware of what you need to do to bring your best self to life.

ZONED IN Acceleration Exercise:

Explain one important event that's coming up and one thing you need to improve in to do your best. For example, if you have to give a presentation to senior leaders, you'll need to practice being articulate. Schedule in a few minutes every night to use imagery training to "practice" speaking articulately. Try to be as detailed as possible.

———————————————————————————

———————————————————————————

———————————————————————————

———————————————————————————

The Not-So-Good News

Imagery training is powerful, so it's important to be highly aware of the recurring thoughts we have and therefore what we practice in our minds. We've just seen the positive effects of imagery training—how it helps us to improve or practice for a high pressure or highly important situation. However, as imagery training can affect our motor control, attention, perception, planning, memory, motivation, confidence, self-efficacy, and progress—what happens when we ruminate on past mistakes or doubt ourselves for the future?

You guessed it! We reinforce and practice the very thing that is causing us so much anguish.

Another client of mine, Jennifer, was recently laid off from a director-level role at her tech company. Despite getting a great severance package and wanting to step away from the long hours and stress of the job, she didn't handle the notice well. Her past few interviews for a new position didn't go so well either. Just like an athlete who is favored to win but loses a few points and is unable to recover, Jennifer felt like she was in a downward spiral.

She wondered what she did wrong to be let go and replayed every poor interaction or project she could remember that didn't go as planned. She thought about her most recent interviews. The more she thought about them, the more emotional she became. "If those interviews didn't go well, how will I ever find a job?" She replayed those limiting beliefs over and over.

The result? Decreased confidence and less motivation in her job search. She was also perfecting her ability to have poor interviews by replaying her errors, rather than learning from them and moving on. Unknowingly, she was using the tool of imagery training to her detriment by:

1. Thinking about the past negative events throughout the day, and therefore increasing her anxiety emotion.

2. Replaying those events at night before bed and when she woke up, which caused her to process these thoughts even in her sleep!

This is an extreme example, but you get the idea. As we'll see in the next chapter, errors and setbacks are valuable, but we need to use them in a certain way. It's not only important to use imagery training to think about how we want to improve in practice or during competition. It's also vital that we're aware of the "movies" we choose to replay, so they help—not hurt—us.

 ## *ZONED IN Acceleration Exercise:*

What is a negative recurring thought you've had in terms of your performance, and how can you switch it to be more positive and encouraging?

_____

_____

The Better News

You have control over how you use imagery training. It's up to you to decide which images you emphasize and practice over and over in your mind. Consistently creating images that help you is a muscle that needs to be flexed over and over to get stronger, especially if you've never done imagery training before, or if you tend to sensationalize events that don't go well. The latter is 100% normal, and it's safe to say that most of us are guilty of it occasionally, but it's time for that to change.

It's time to write the scripts for the movies we *want* to play and choose to play *that* script over and over. We must pull out the good, redirect the not-so-good, and know how to navigate the images created by nay-sayers and negative people in our lives. Just like an Olympian, we can direct our images to accelerate our progress and see the success we want and deserve.

This alone isn't enough though. Ultimately, personal success is a collaboration of resilient optimists who push each other beyond the comfort zone—not just set goals, but to dream big. We must challenge each other to dream bigger, and believe whatever is in each of our hearts, we can achieve. We must help each other paint pictures of our future ambitions, which maybe we can't even see. We should ask each other "What do those ambitions look like, and why haven't you acted yet?" Sometimes, we need help creating images that will support our future ambitions, so we can rise together.

For now, the first step is raising awareness of the results you desire and knowing how to shift back to them, especially during missteps or setbacks. This means knowing how to choose which movies to create and replay. In the next section, you'll see how to become the director of your images and construct images that play a supporting role in your success.

ZONED IN Acceleration Exercise:

Write about a current event that you're preparing for (or a past event) where you've replayed a negative thought over and over in your mind. How might this negative imagery training be impacting your progress and how can you reframe this thought to help you improve?

_____

_____

_____

_____

_____

The Power of Sequencing

If imagery training is the entire movie, _sequencing_ is the trailer of the most important parts. The short clips that you can use to focus on what matters most. Now you understand how powerful our repetitive thoughts can be—and the importance of guiding them towards what we want to achieve, rather than replaying past worries or failures. But what's the best way to create the actual images that will serve our success? A great way to get this done is sequencing, a tool I use with world-class athletes to help them with skill acquisition. By the end of this section, you'll be able to use sequencing to improve in whatever skill is most important to you.

Think of a sequence as being your set of short movie clips that will become the sizzle reel of your success. However, it's important to be aware of a couple challenges here. Notably, our brains have a similar limitation to monkeys! Our working memory is comparable to theirs, even though a monkey's brain is a fraction of the size. Humans are at a slight advantage in being able to hold on average four different pieces of information in their working memory, compared to three-to-four for a monkey. This means we can't work on many different areas at once.[41] So, when using sequencing, it's important to consider focusing on just three things.

Think about how phone numbers are broken up. For example, in the United States, a phone number may look like 555-555-1212. The hyphens allow us to group the numbers, so we memorize three chunks, rather than ten individual digits. This working memory hack can help us create images we'll remember more easily. When it comes to improving a skill, sequencing is a similar technique to break up a pattern of skill acquisition.[42]

How to Use Sequencing

If you want to be the award-winning producer of your next big win, you need to know how to create short films that add up to your success. Sequencing is a way to use chunks of information either before you "compete" or to reinforce your performance after you finish. Specifically, sequences are short movie clips that direct your attention to the three most important items you are trying to become proficient at. This is a way of practicing in your mind in addition to physically practicing. Sequencing helps you decide which film is important and is included in the main event, and which film ends up on the cutting room floor.

Let's say you're a world-class track and field athlete training for an upcoming 100m sprint. Your goal is to drop two-tenths of a second in the next two weeks. Sequencing is a great way to use your limited time on the track to drop time. A way to dial into what you must master to fun faster. A way to practice when you're not physically running.

When reviewing your technique, let's say your coach tells you it's your start that needs the most improvement. For the next two weeks, you're laser-focused on nailing the three technical aspects of your start. They are:

1. Upper body begins at 45 degrees.

2. Push forward for the first four strides.

3. Strong arms.

You can group this information more simply by thinking "upper body, push, arms." Your ability to extract what's most important then assign importance to the three words will help you create and execute a winning mini-movie of your best efforts—a sequence.

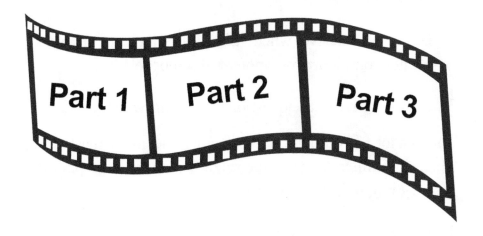

In the beginning, you may want to consider breaking your sequence down into three parts, mastering each part, and then putting the entire sequence together. For example, the track athlete may practice starting the race with her upper body at 45 degrees for many repetitions until mastery before moving on to the other two parts of the sequence. Although most adults are perfectly capable of holding three pieces of information in working memory, it can be highly beneficial to be a true monotasker to master one part of the sequence at a time first.[43]

Let's take Jennifer from our earlier example. After gaining the courage to ask her past two interviewers for feedback, Jennifer received three valuable pieces of advice to prepare for her upcoming interviews. They were:

1. **Be more energetic,** because she appeared disinterested in the position.

2. **Be more decisive** when asked questions to project greater confidence for a potential senior role.

3. **Listen better** to the questions before answering.

This is a lot of information to remember, let alone master. So, I helped Jennifer create an interview sequence for preparation before going into future interviews:

1. **Energy.**

2. **Decisive.**

3. **Listen.**

She practiced each one, just like Olympians do, in her mind. She saw herself take a few deep breaths before her interview to get focused and generate the energy she needed. She saw herself answering questions decisively and practiced her eye contact. She saw herself waiting until the interviewer finished speaking before she responded. Through this interview sequence, Jennifer practiced for her next interview before it happened. She mastered the input she was given and made sure that a successful interview was familiar to her.

These three things proved useful for a few reasons. First, all three components of her interview sequence were under her control, which helped Jennifer feel more in control, confident, and relaxed. Second, they directed her attention towards what was most important, therefore giving her the best shot at the desired outcome. It's important to note here the key difference compared to long-term objectives where we assume the desired result will happen, then relinquish control.

ZONED IN Acceleration Exercise:

Create a sequence to practice for an upcoming event.

_____

_____

_____

_____

_____

How to Think in HD and Bring Your Movie to Life

Jennifer prepared for an upcoming interview by visiting a friend's office and having her friend ask a few questions similar to those Jennifer had been asked in previous interviews. After the first few questions, Jennifer recognized that her energy was only around five out of ten, and it needed to be closer to seven.

She took a deep breath in through her nose and exhaled through her mouth. Then she answered the question again, with much more energy, enthusiasm, and engagement. Each time she answered a question with a level seven energy and engagement, she reinforced it by thinking, "Yes, that's it!"

As we saw in Chapter 5, emotions are powerful. Consequently, they play a powerful role in imagery training. Jennifer did a great job of creating high-resolution HD movies of what was most important for her. That way, she could have a successful interview by placing high emotion on what she did correctly.

Whether it's world-class athletes or us, the imagery training that produces the most effective results is more than just visual.[43] The sights, sounds, physical feelings, thoughts, and emotions of an actual "competition" are important too. Thinking about a sequence is a good start—but *feeling* and physically experiencing it is better.

For example, it's common for an equestrian show-jumping athlete to "walk the course" of fences before a competition. This enables the rider to better understand the complexity of the turns, the distance between jumps, and opportunities to cut time on the course. To use these few precious moments in the most impactful way, critical parts of the course must be in HD or extremely vivid and multi-sensory. What are the smells in the arena? What are the colors of the different fences? What noises are present? How does it feel to sink into the saddle and close your fingers around the reins, which asks the horse to shorten his stride?

Walking a course is an opportunity to create sequences and bring them to life by taking in the smell of the arena, the colors of the jumps, the sounds of the crowd, and the critical components of how to maneuver the course. Finally, the rider can create the emotion and joy associated with clearing the final jump, rewarding the horse with a pat on the neck, and knowing they just edged out their closest competitor to win.

Let's step out of the arena and into the conference room. How can you bring an important presentation or pitch to life before it happens, so you have your best shot at emerging as a champion? Ideally, you'd be able to "walk the course" too. In other words, spend time in the conference room where you'll be presenting. The more realistic you can make it, the better. Bring your PowerPoint and a couple of colleagues with you, then practice like it's the real presentation.

Although experiencing the actual venue and an audience isn't always realistic, it's important to practice in a way that's as realistic as possible. You may have to improvise here, for example, use a different conference room if the real room isn't available. If this isn't realistic either, create the environment for yourself in your mind. Who will be attending? Where will they sit? What potential questions might they ask? Mentally place them in the room before you begin. Speak to them, connect with their eyes, answer their questions, and get across your most important points while you're practicing.

Doing this makes all the difference in how effective your imagery training is. Without these details, the images aren't stored well in your memory, resulting in a pixelated movie when you try to recall it for your imagery training. If you can assign a high level of detail, vividness, and emotion to your practice, then your movies will be in HD, making them easier and clearer to recall—as we saw in Chapter 5.

The result? You're more likely to be familiar with your surroundings, more relaxed, and more confident when the big day comes.

ZONED IN Acceleration Exercise:

What are a couple vivid details for an upcoming important event or interaction that you can practice using imagery training?

_____

_____

_____

_____

_____

Rewinding errors to create success

So, you know how to create HD images to form sequences for imagery training, and this should help you accelerate your proficiency. But you may be wondering, what happens when you mess up during practice? Do you fast-forward and keep going—or hit replay and try again?

There is a definite difference between performing in real-time and practicing. During an actual competition, the show must go on, and most of the time, we just must push forward. Practicing is different in that we can "replay," erase the error, and replace it with a new, more accurate rendition. This is a key component of creating the most useful images for your sequences. When you slip up in practice, you can when possible:

1. **Stop** what you're doing.

2. **Rewind** the clip to before you started.

3. **Start again** and see yourself doing the task the right way.

Remember to "rewind" as soon as possible after making an error. For Jennifer, she answered the first question, refocused, then answered the same question again. When done correctly, this can have the same effect as doing your best in the first place. Replaying the sequence right after you execute it correctly is important too, because it's very fresh in your mind.[44]

 ZONED IN Acceleration Exercise:

Think of a recent error you made at work, in your sport, or during a crucial conversation. What was it? How could you rewind it and make it a success, so you can improve for next time?

_____

_____

_____

_____

The Next Level of Imagery Training

Seeing is believing, literally. Mastering and applying imagery training will not guarantee your success, but it will help you believe what you want is possible and motivate you to keep trying. World-class imagery training is not just reserved for high-level athletes. If we can utilize a few more specific and simple details, we too can practice and "compete" better. These details will help you believe and make the most out of the time you spend on and off the "field." Here's how:

1. **Create** conditions that are somewhat realistic: If your presentation or interview is likely be moderately challenging, don't put yourself through a series of grueling sequences where you're being fired questions and raked over the coals when practicing. Similarly, don't be too easy on yourself either. The more similar the imagined conditions are to the real ones you're likely to experience, the better.[45]

2. **Imagine** a performance that is somewhat realistic: Sometimes, I imagine that I'm sitting with Oprah discussing my book. At least for now, that performance is not realistic. I'm all about dreaming BIG, but when preparing for an upcoming event—it's important to imagine yourself preparing for your next most-important performance. In my case, it's presenting to a group of female leaders in a prominent investment banking firm in San Francisco. I want to hit it out of the park

for them, so these are the sequences I'm creating and practicing:

- **Connect** with them by taking an interest in their challenges.

- **Listen** to them.

- **Deliver** content that will serve them on their quest to achieve the success and joy they want and deserve.

After we've had a champion performance on our most current important event, there's time to dream about the conversation with Oprah, or whatever goal makes you happy and proud. When it's game time, it's time to get present focus of our highest level of service and inspiration on the task at hand.

3. **Set imagery parameters to follow.** Back in Chapter 3, you learned that effective short-term objectives are specific in time, place, duration, and effort. When preparing for an upcoming event, this holds true as well.

- When will you practice your most important sequences (i.e. which days and what time)?

- How long will you practice?

- Where will you practice?

- What level of focus will you have on a scale of 1-10, 1 being very distracted and 10 being laser focused?

For example, when preparing for an upcoming presentation, you might set these parameters: "I will arrive at work 15 minutes early every day this week to physically practice in the conference room where I'll be presenting and then run through my closing argument sequence. I will also take a couple minutes every night before bed to practice this same sequence five times."

 ## ZONED IN Acceleration Exercise:

Write one way you can create a somewhat realistic condition (for example, where you'll practice and who will be present) and how you will set the parameters (time, place, duration, and effort) to use your imagery training.

_____

_____

_____

_____

_____

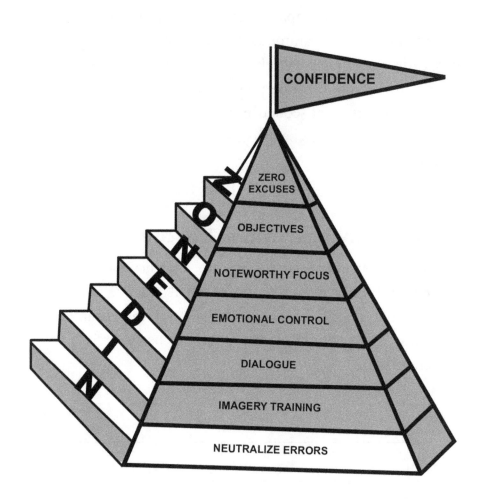

Chapter 8

NEUTRALIZING
AND UTILIZING ERRORS

The Secret Weapon to Your Success

"It's not about the actual failure itself, it's how you respond to it." – Abby Wambach

On our quest to achieve beyond our current circumstances, there's a great neutralizer: we are *all* going to make mistakes and fail. From what I have experienced over the years—success favors those who are most agile in responding to errors.

Famous Failures and Future Successes

In addition, there are countless stories in history of those who have failed, some quite significantly, before realizing their ultimate success. One of my personal favorites is Thomas

Edison. At one point, his teacher told him he was "too stupid to learn anything." He also was fired from his first two jobs for not being productive enough, not to mention his thousand-plus failed attempts at inventing the lightbulb. Edison had this response when asked how it felt to fail so many times: "I didn't fail 1,000 times. The light bulb was an invention with 1,000 steps."[46]

Let's take modern-day media mogul Arianna Huffington, who has among other epic accomplishments written 13 books and created an unparalleled media empire. But despite all of her truly amazing achievements, she has also made mistakes along the way. In fact, she ran for governor of California back in 2003, made some key errors, and failed.

However, she described the experience as being one that she learned a lot from. It also had a great impact on her forming the *Huffington Post*, from seeing the power of the internet to learning the importance of communication and listening. Her mother couldn't have said it better when she advised Arianna, "Failure is a stepping-stone to success."[47] In this chapter, we'll put this timeless advice to work.

Consider Oprah, who moved on to start her own network: OWN (the Oprah Winfrey Network) after 21 seasons of having a number one show. As she explained in her 2013 Harvard University commencement speech, "Nearly every media outlet proclaimed it a flop." Reading the *USA Today* headline "Oprah Winfrey Isn't Quite Holding Her OWN" was particularly memorable for her.[48] Although she proclaimed this was a low in her professional career, she told the Harvard graduates that she *would* turn her network around. And she did.

Whether you're at the pinnacle of your career, trying something new, or climbing towards the next level of your current ambition, I believe everyone has their own individual achievements that are no less important than winning an influential political race or building a media empire. If errors are a great neutralizer, so is the way we perceive and use them when marching to our next big win. If you know what to do with errors, you'll recover from them, improve quicker, and compete better when the pressure is on.

It's time to make our ambitions greater than our fear of making mistakes. To be at peace with errors, and ask them to stand with us rather than allowing them to push us out of the arena, leaving us defeated. Like an athlete after a poor performance, we must allow a brief mourning period, then get curious, and be determined to improve. We must learn to be resilient. The good news is that we absolutely *can*, and you'll learn some of the tools to do just that in this chapter.

Step Outside Your Comfort Zone

As explained by the world's leading expert on expertise, K. Anders Ericsson, if you're *not* making errors, then you're not pushing yourself outside your comfort zone, which is a key factor in reaching your next level of success.[49] Simply going about our regular comfortable routine when trying to reach a new level of success isn't enough. Nor is just being at peace with whatever mistakes we make. Instead, we must intentionally seek out challenging situations that are necessary for our growth, says Ericsson—even where we are *likely* to make errors. I will be the first to admit, this can be terrifying.

A few years back, I was asked to sit on a panel for an event that would be internationally broadcasted. It was hosted by a major technology firm in San Francisco for a group of accomplished female technologists. One panelist was a 30 Under 30 technologist and the other was a consultant to many C-suite executives in San Francisco and Silicon Valley.

At the time, I was working exclusively with high-level teens, college, and pre-Olympic athletes—not women who have built multiple successful companies. I politely thanked the invitee and declined. After all, who was I to be speaking to a group of powerful and influential women? My area of expertise was essentially working with clients the same ages as their children! Full transparency, I was afraid. Afraid that I would get dwarfed by the other panelists and not be able to add value to the extremely successful attendees' lives.

Thankfully, the coordinator was persistent, and I eventually agreed. I have immense gratitude to her every day, because that one event changed my career forever. I got pushed way outside my comfort zone. In retrospect, walking away from that opportunity is unthinkable now. To achieve the next level of success, it's often necessary to lean *into* the next level of discomfort, even when it's likely that you'll make mistakes along the way.

I decided to get busy learning what these women needed, and what they struggled with, especially when they had to pitch their companies to then-predominately-male venture capitalists. Like an athlete who commits to being all in on her quest to be the best, I decided to be all in too. I got laser-focused on finding answers to these important questions, and preparing to serve these women with potentially unfamiliar content—yet important tools for their already impressive tool belt. There was no permission given. In many cases, mental toughness is the ability to give permission to yourself. The engagement for this event was astonishing, and my business was forever changed. I experienced a level of joy that comes with accomplishing something that did not seem possible at first.

Whether you're not sure what your next big win is yet, if you're beginning your journey towards something meaningful, or you've already arrived and are striving for an even higher level of ambition—either way, I wish the same joy for you and the ripple effect it will have on those who matter most to you.

So, how can the emotions associated with stepping outside your comfort zone and making errors, give us power rather than diminish it?

1. **Gain perspective on errors,** especially for women.

2. **Pull errors closer** rather than push them away to extract their power.

3. **Have error amnesia.**

This is a different way of thinking and doing. But it is completely achievable, and you'll see the way to do this in the coming sections. First, let's see where you are willing go.

 ZONED IN Acceleration Exercise:

What is one way you can step outside your comfort zone and make progress towards your next win? What error or mistakes are you afraid of making, and do you agree to proceed anyway?

_____

_____

_____

_____

A Word on Women and Errors

Some not-so-good news is that women are often up against obstacles not as prevalent for our male counterparts.[50] On top of this, in many cultures, women are engrained from a young age to have a counterproductive chatter in their own mind about errors and failure. There may be a more technical or sophisticated name, but I call it the "itty bitty shitty committee."

The way we communicate errors to ourselves and others is explored by Dr. Martin Seligman in his book *Learned Optimism*. Often referred to as "the father of positive psychology," Dr. Seligman is a world-renowned researcher and expert in the areas of learned helplessness, optimism, and pessimism. His work sheds light on why this obstacle exists for women, the consequences of not addressing it, and ways to undo some of the roadblocks created for women in our youth. These revelations aren't just important for us, but also for those we influence at work and at home.

Seligman explains that early in life, our "explanatory style" begins to form. This means how we communicate with ourselves, particularly when it comes to mistakes and failures. He points out that children have keen ears—not only to *what* we say, but *how* we say it. This is relevant both in terms of thinking about how we were brought up, and how we speak to the children in our lives now. According to Seligman, the words we hear over and over as we grow up can have a profound effect on how we perceive setbacks, particularly before adolescence and from our mothers.

Seligman found that a mother and her child's level of optimism is similar, especially in perceiving errors and setbacks.

If a mother is pessimistic in explaining a setback or failure to herself, then her child is likely to view their setbacks in the same way. Likewise, if she explains the error in a way that isn't an isolated incident, for example, "I always get overlooked for promotions" or in a way that is personal, for example, "There must be something wrong with me," the child may adapt this explanatory style too.

This is compounded when children are criticized in the same way for errors they make. For children, it makes their mistakes seem like mountains that are impossible to climb. Similarly, Carol Dweck, leading researcher in emotional development, found that girls who were given impossible problems to solve typically explained their failures as permanent and personal. For example, "I'm not very good at math" or "I'm not very smart." On the other hand, boys often responded to failure by saying "I didn't try very hard" or "I wasn't paying attention," which is in their control.

Now, as adults, what does this mean for us when we make a mistake or fail? Is it possible that we sometimes feel we are not capable, smart enough, or worthy based on how we were raised or based on what we heard repeatedly in our youth? If so, how does it influence the way we communicate with girls we're role models for if we do not believe in ourselves?

Fortunately, we can take control of how we perceive errors or the possibility of making errors. First, we should be aware of what we tell ourselves when we make an error. In the earlier example, after Jennifer had a few poor interviews, she learned to explain her setbacks as temporary: *"That interview* didn't go very well" and not personal, "I must not be right for *that job."* Rather than permanent: *"I'm never* going to get a job" or personal: *"I'm* a *terrible* candidate."

Second, we need to be aware of how we explain setbacks to others, especially the children in our lives. Thanks to Carol Dweck's lifetime of research, we have a better understanding of how to help others develop optimism and resilience. Like Seligman, she found that it all starts with what kids hear repetitively, from their parents, teachers and other influential adults in their lives. And letting them know that errors and mistakes are temporary, not personal or innate, and not permanent.

Third, we must make a conscious effort to explain errors as less of a permanent condition and more of a *journey* to success. This takes consistent practice until it becomes a habit. If you throw your hat in the ring for a new job and get rejected, are you truly incapable of landing a new job, or can you learn from the experience? It's time to understand and decide that errors are here to stay, and we must learn how to work with them.

Managing Your Inner McEnroe

When you make an error, how you respond is crucial. As we saw in Chapter 5, in any arena there are the John McEnroes of the world, who lose their composure after an error. Although there's no doubt that McEnroe was a legend in his sport, there were consequences to his outbursts. During the 1990 Australian Open, unknown to McEnroe, the rules were changed for the number of code violations that resulted in disqualification. This fourth outburst resulted in McEnroe being the first tennis player in the Open Era to be ejected from a Grand Slam.[51]

However, outbursts like this in our career are not likely to be as amusing or well-tolerated. In general, world-class athletes who are consistently at top of their sport for the long haul (like Roger Federer) are remarkably composed after errors, and we need to be too. Just like world-class athletes whose lives and livelihoods are centered around their sport, what you're working toward is extremely important too. Errors can certainly be helpful on your journey, but they can also be harmful to your performance if not handled in a certain way. Before learning how to use errors in the right way, let's look at how *not* to treat errors.

First, make sure you're not over-punishing yourself for your crime. In other words, when you make an error, be realistic about the impact, and don't sensationalize or overthink it, especially in high-pressure or highly important situations. Errors are rarely as fatal as we build them up to be. If you can hold a snowball in your hand, does it make sense to build it into an avalanche in your mind? If you do, you may start on a downward spiral and find yourself at the bottom of the mountain.[52]

This is how the less-experienced player can rise to be victorious over the more talented player. One has nothing to lose, recovers quickly, and gives 100% even after errors or setbacks. The other stokes the errors with self-inflicted fuel. After making an error, it may be helpful to ask yourself, "What is the real consequence of this error?" or "Is this the correct perspective, and am I being fair to myself?" It's certainly okay to be disappointed after an error, and it would be a much bigger problem if you didn't care, but having perspective on the *magnitude* of an error is key to recovery. If it is truly a huge deal, take some time to feel the emotions associated with the error, then decide on a strategy to move on.

Second, be careful of perceiving your error as a threat to your outcome, as perception of errors can greatly impact results. Errors typically become threats when they are associated too much with outcomes such as winning potential business, approval of peers or managers, or a reward of some type. It's like missing three baskets in basketball and thinking of it as a threat to losing the game. The result of doing so can be performance-related anxiety and other physical symptoms that get in the way of achieving champion results.

There are many other factors associated with the outcome of the game than just three baskets, and you personally don't have control over losing the game. It's more productive to take control of your response and think of the error as a challenge. This can help you enjoy the process more and take a position of authority over yourself to improve.

What's more, challenging yourself to improve after an error can instill greater confidence. It can also direct your attention toward what you need to do for the best possible result, rather than ruminating about what you did wrong.[53]

ZONED IN Acceleration Exercise:

Imagine you make an error in an important meeting. What question can you ask yourself to keep your error in perspective?

_____

_____

_____

_____

_____

Ally vs. Enemy

How do we make an error or have a setback, then dust ourselves off and keep moving forward? The answer is to use the error as an ally rather than look at is as an enemy. Rather than dwell on errors, ask yourself: "What did I learn, and how do I want this to turn out? This sets your sights on future ambitions rather than current circumstances, and helps to figure out the next most important course of action to improve. Errors can be used to take control rather than to be controlling. We have a choice for our perspective and for our reaction to errors.

Errors aren't just your teacher then—they can also be the fuel to recover quickly and with a vengeance, so it's important to pull them closer and not push them away. We can choose the hat that we want our errors to wear. Once we learn from them, errors can be the coach, teammate, colleague or friend, cheering with all their heart.

Learning how to harness the power of errors to not just recover—but to amplify our efforts can propel us forward when we might otherwise slow down or worse, quit. When we practice and develop this mental toughness, we can even look errors in the face from a place of gratitude.

 ## ZONED IN Acceleration Exercise:

What is one way you can pull an error closer? What can you learn from it?

_____

_____

_____

_____

Error Amnesia

Have you ever made a mistake, had a setback or experienced a misstep only to have it happen over and over? Whether a tennis player who misses a string of first serves, a salesperson who gets rejected over and over by prospects, or a couple failed attempts getting on a fitness routine, learning how to eventually release errors is an important part of the mental toughness puzzle.

Once we pull errors closer to learn, recover, or grow, we must then release them from our conscious thought in an effort to have error amnesia. Amnesia certainly isn't a condition that's typically desirable, but in the case of error recovery, it can come in handy. Negative thoughts surrounding errors are common, but they're not very productive if held onto for too long. As covered in Chapter 5, errors are at best distracting and at worst can trigger negative emotions and therefore impede performance.

Unknowingly, when we ruminate about errors, we are reinforcing the very things we *do not* want to repeat. Instead, it's better to make peace with errors and move them aside—to make room for more constructive thoughts. Do you remember the "release" portion of the emotional wheel in Chapter 5? Error amnesia is closely tied to this step of managing emotions. A small yet important detail to note is that we are *releasing* the error out of our conscious thought—not getting rid of it. Think of an error like a cloud that floats by.

Here's the difference: the harder we try to shove something out of our head (i.e. not think about the pink elephant in the room), the more we tend to think about it.[54] It simply does not work. Having error amnesia and releasing an error from our mind is *imagining it moving aside*. It's then making space for a thought that will serve your efforts. What if this is simply not possible? If you must set aside time to feel an error, to be frustrated about it or deal with it more, you can absolutely do that as long it is not during 'competition'. However, it's important to realize that there is an appropriate and inappropriate time to think about errors, and during practice or competition is *not one of them*. Even so, the more efficient we can get at pulling errors closer, learning and then letting them go, the more agile we'll be on our climb.

Like anything else, this takes practice. So, try this the next time you catch yourself dwelling on an error:

1. **Stop:** Say "Stop" to yourself to disrupt any future thoughts about your error.

2. **Ask:** What was the correct way? How do I need to adjust?

3. **Forget:** Breath in and breath out, releasing the error on our exhale. What about any emotional leftovers after you stop, ask and forget? *Use it!* For decades, it was common practice to coach athletes to be calm, carefree (of the outcome), and focused on the task at hand.

That still rings true, but there is an important next step that can help your performance:

4. **Redirect:** Send the emotion from your error back towards what you need to be doing correctly. Emotions are powerful, and it's important that you keep putting them to good use until they are released.

Let's say you are the track athlete who fails to dig out of the blocks during the 400m. After a few not-so-ideal strides and seeing the competition pull away, you can redirect the negative emotion from worrying about the error to immediately redirecting it and thinking "Dig!" The same with the next presentation you have. If you stumble out of the gate or in the middle, stop the thought, ask what is the correct way, forget the error by taking deep breath and releasing it, redirect any residual emotion towards your best performance. You can use residual emotion to make up lost ground and win your race by investing it in the desired performance rather than ruminating about your current circumstance.

ZONED IN Acceleration Exercise:

Think of a past error you made. It might be in a conversation, presentation, pitch, or any other event that was important to you. What did you think after it happened? How could you SAFR (stop, ask, forget, redirect) instead of suffer?

_____

_____

_____

_____

_____

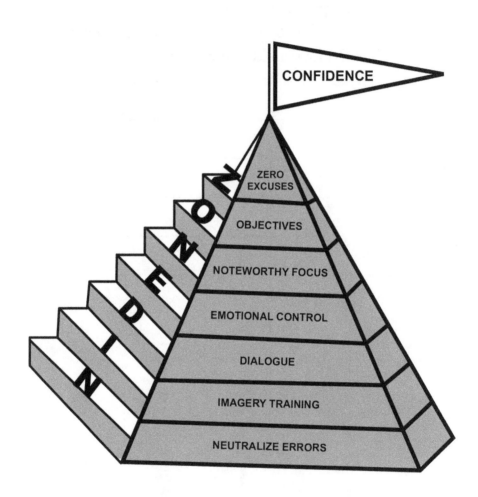

Chapter 9

CONFIDENCE

Bringing It All Together

Congratulations on making it through the ZONED IN Mental Toughness Framework! I hope you found the world-class tips, tools, and habits useful, and you can apply them to practice and perform at your best—especially in those important moments. As you move from understanding to mastering to applying the seven steps of becoming ZONED IN, you'll build the confidence required to dream big, accelerate progress, and perform under pressure.

Confidence is even more important than you may realize. Scott Barry Kaufman, PhD, a cognitive psychologist, author, podcaster, and professor at the University of Pennsylvania, has dedicated his life to studying how we can live our most creative, fulfilling, and meaningful lives. Dr. Kaufman explains in a recent article in *Psychology Today*:

"A bulk of research shows that when people are put in situations where they are expected to fail, their performance does plummet. They turn into different people. Their head literally shuts down, and they end up confirming the expectations. When they're expected to win, their performance shoots back up. Same person, difference expectations."[55]

Having the confidence to perform well doesn't mean we know definitively that we're always going to win or come out on top. It does mean that we make a conscious decision to proceed as if our desired result will happen, and we take the consistent necessary steps as if we "are on a path" to that end. It also means that we have an unwavering belief in the possibility of arriving at our destination and commit to making progress towards what we yearn for. This confidence in ourselves matters, especially when our journey gets difficult, in the moments when we are tested, to see how badly we want to claim victory.

The components of the ZONED IN mental toughness acronym are intimately related, and one is no less important than the other. Now we'll see how each step is related to the other and how each helps to build your confidence.

Zero Excuses

When you set up an accountability structure for yourself and learn to have zero excuses, it's like a world-class athlete who is working toward her big dream. She views every workout as vital to her long-term success. She has a system in place to make sure workouts get done, even on the hard days when the temptation to skip a session is strong.

Although it's vital to ultimately have self-accountability, we also need a team to support us, and I encourage you to form yours. Take inventory of your current circumstances and what support you need. For example, if you are in the process in getting into the best shape of your life, do you know what exercises to do, and how to do them safely? What about your nutrition? Do you know how to best fuel your body? What if you are gunning for that raise, scaling your business or preparing for a crucial conversation?

Your Zero Excuses team can be a formal structure within your company, provided by an independent coach, or it can be far less formal. Whichever system works for you is the right system, and it's very important to form a support system for your confidence and for your success. Who will cheer you on or provide guidance when you are struggling? Who will you celebrate with? Who will challenge you when your ambitions don't match up with your actions?

We all need someone on our own personal board of directors to collaborate with us, challenge us, and guide us when we push towards uncharted territories of success. Someone who has confidence in us when we're in the process of building confidence in ourselves.

ZONED IN Acceleration Exercise:

What is most important to you right now, and where do you need the most help? Who might be able to help you? When will you reach out to that person?

_____

_____

_____

_____

_____

Objectives

Objectives and zero excuses are like fraternal twins. Having an accountability structure in place will make you more likely to meet your objectives. It will help you go the extra mile on those days when it's much easier not to take those small steps.

If you have objectives but make excuses, it's a recipe for mediocrity, and that's not where progress and optimal performance live. Confidence is built on small successes, and it's the short-term objectives that add up to your long-term success. You're more likely to take those small but important steps consistently when you are accountable to yourself and to others.[56]

ZONED IN Acceleration Exercise:

What small win or progress will you commit to consistently? Who will hold you accountable? What will your confidence level be on a scale of 1-10, 1 not being confident at all and 10 being extremely confident, if you succeed?

_____

_____

_____

_____

_____

Noteworthy Focus

Considering the average worker switches tasks every three minutes and distractions are more prevalent than ever, not having strategies to focus can be costly and frustrating.[57] Once you've planned for your long, intermediate, and short-term objectives and set up an accountability structure to make consistent progress more likely, it's important that you learn to focus more efficiently during practice and competition.

Having noteworthy focus is directly related to confidence, because you can choose to direct your thoughts during tasks that you have control over, rather than perceived obstacles that are out of your control. For example, when preparing for a presentation, you can choose what is most important to think about, such as energy level or eye contact. Will you choose to focus on those things or what could go wrong? World-class performers know how to master their focus to ensure optimal progress and optimal performance under pressure, and so can you.

 ## *ZONED IN Acceleration Exercise:*

What is an upcoming important event you have? What controllable thing will you choose to focus on? How will this affect your confidence?

_____

_____

_____

_____

Emotional Control

Whether you're competing with yourself or others, on the field or in the boardroom, how you manage your emotions and choose to perceive events matters. Although it's extremely normal to attach a lot of emotion to events perceived as negative, it isn't helpful for your confidence or your future performance.

For example, a tennis player double-faults for the second time in a row or a sales executive delivers a presentation that is not well-received. Those events may produce a high level of doubt (in their ability), fear (of failing again or fear of what others think), and frustration (at the lack of results). These negative thoughts tend to be a detriment to your confidence, but they *are* controllable.[58] The show must go on, and so must your ability to take control of your thoughts and emotions.

Remember the emotional wheel? If you have a lack of awareness, emotional agility, and emotional control, it results in your negative emotions gaining more power than they deserve or warrant. That's when you find yourself in the red zone. Confidence and your best performance do not live in this dangerous place, especially during a big game. Learning how to manage and control your emotions will give you the confidence you need to get back in the green and become ZONED IN.

 ## ZONED IN Acceleration Exercise:

What is the most impactful thing that has resonated with you about emotional control, how will you implement it, and how will it affect your confidence?

_____

_____

_____

_____

Dialogue

The person we converse with the most is ourselves, and we tend to believe what we consistently hear.[59] Whether you're an Olympian or a recreational athlete, a C-suite executive or on the climb, the dialogue you have with yourself can determine the confidence you foster or disable.

Your internal voice or dialogue can help you maneuver through failure and setbacks. It can guide you towards triumphs, both large and small. In turn, you can become more confident in your ability to recover quickly from errors and forge ahead when doubt is knocking at your door.

 ZONED IN Acceleration Exercise:

What's one way your dialogue can be more positive and encouraging? How would this help your confidence?

_____

_____

_____

_____

Imagery Training

This advanced tool used by world-class athletes accelerates our progress and helps us perform successfully under pressure. The dialogue we have with ourselves and the emotion we create is the foundation for the micro-movies or sequences we think about over and over during imagery training. Whether you're an Olympic hopeful or hoping to get a raise, imagery training can help you prepare and compete optimally. You can also gain confidence by achieving small wins in your mind and making high-pressure environments familiar.

Now you have the tools to be ZONED IN, plan for your success, manage which thoughts to focus on, manage the emotions associated with errors and setbacks, and create a dialogue with yourself that will support your success. These tools will give you a world-class level of heightened awareness and control over your imagery training. Ultimately, control over what you choose to improve.

Whether at home, at work, or for your sport, you can now combine real-time practice with imagery training to build competency and confidence.

🏅 *ZONED IN Acceleration Exercise:*

What is something you could practice using imagery training? How could this help your confidence?

_____

_____

_____

_____

_____

Neutralizing and Utilizing Errors

Being able to neutralize and utilize errors is like finding a pocket full of twenty-dollar bills that you never knew you had. Errors at any level of proficiency are inevitable, but they are also invaluable. It's my sincere hope that by now you've had a mindset shift around errors. Hopefully, errors are no longer the evil villain, but instead the ally who provides tough love for you to grow and improve.

Noteworthy focus, emotional control, dialogue, and imagery training—when used in synchronicity—are the catalysts for neutralizing and utilizing errors. You have power to choose what you focus on, manage and utilize your emotions, optimally converse with yourself, and practice an event in your mind. Now you can decide what errors mean to you, and whether they will be a friend or foe.

When errors happen, your ability to bring them closer, listen to them, and use them to be agile will create confidence. The mindset shift surrounding errors may give you the confidence to try something you've been yearning to do, have the difficult conversation you've been putting off, or throw your hat in an arena for a position you've only dreamed about before. Making peace with errors and learning how to view them as one of your biggest supporters can give you the confidence to reach the next level of success.

 ## ZONED IN Acceleration Exercise:

When have you made an error? How is it holding you back now? What did you learn from this error? How can you use it to improve?

_____

_____

_____

_____

_____

THE MOST IMPORTANT TAKEAWAYS

Learning how to be ZONED IN is a marathon, not a sprint. It's about planning for what you want and having the mental toughness to make consistent progress and compete in the moments that matter most. If there are three things I'd like you to be certain of and remember, they are:

1. You are only limited by what you think is possible.

2. The confidence you need to achieve what you yearn for is a learned skill.

3. If no one else believes in you, I absolutely do.

I've seen the transformation in myself, my children, and countless clients, and I absolutely believe that what you desire is possible for you too!

Confidence will give you hope, the nudge to take a chance on something important, and importantly the ability to show up and be a champion after all the hard work and preparation. Here is an example of someone who was confident, and how his confidence manifested in himself and others.

Before Roger Banister ran a sub-four-minute mile, no one thought it was possible. Trying such a feat was viewed as ludicrous. But in 1954, Banister ran a sub-four-minute mile, and shortly after, his record was broken by other men—who even ran it a little faster.

What does this mean for you if you're not a runner? Your belief in yourself that you *can* achieve something (your self-efficacy) and your confidence is incredibly important when it comes to achieving that thing. Roger Banister *believed* he could run a sub-four-minute mile, and he *did*.[60] Were the runners after Banister blessed with different athletic capabilities all of the sudden? Or were they now confident in their ability because someone else had achieved the impossible? Does this story change what you think is possible?

The first step of being ZONED IN is believing what you want is *possible*. Are there any limitations that you put on yourself that possibly don't exist or that can be overcome? Then it's time to think about how you'll stand up to fear and doubt.

It's time to use the tools you've learned in this book to forge ahead into uncharted territory. To achieve the success and joy you want and deserve. It's time to think about what *your* four-minute mile is, to get ZONED IN, and to start thinking like you are the champion you wish to become.

Like all of those who ran a sub-four-minute mile after Roger Banister, who will your success impact and empower after you arrive at your next finish line? Who are you a role model for, and who do you influence? You may be surprised at the potential ripple effect under your control.

ZONED IN Acceleration Exercise:

What is one new perspective you've gained on an important ambition? What action are you going to take because of it?

_____

_____

_____

_____

YOU now have the tools to be ZONED IN, and I honor you for being one of the ambitious and dedicated people who read a book cover to cover. This in and of itself puts you in an elite class of achievers. It means that you are serious about learning how to access the mental toughness required to be the best version of yourself. For you, for those who matter most now, and for those who you haven't even met yet. For those who are waiting for your light to shine and for those who are waiting for the special gift that is uniquely yours.

You're off to an amazing start, but mastering and applying these tools goes beyond this book. I'd like to make this content real for you and help you along the way to your next level of success and joy. So, here's where I hand on the baton. I'm including a wealth of resources for you to continue your mental toughness journey.

"I believe in you always, and you can achieve whatever you put your mind to."

With deepest gratitude for you and with total confidence in you,

Sheryl

ACKNOWLEDGEMENTS

This book was born from struggle and frustration as a young person as well as my desire to help others to be confident and resilient, and to perform under pressure. My curiosity about how world-class athletes could be mentally tough, so they could show up and deliver their best under the most intense circumstances, lead to a belief and a mission that we can all learn the same tools—to be ZONED IN. This book took an immense amount of work, and it would not have been possible without the invaluable contributions of a few incredibly thoughtful, brilliant, and supportive people, including:

My father, Cecil Louis Kline. We all need someone to believe in us, and my father believed in me every day. Whether in school, in my sport, or early in my career, he always told me I was capable of accomplishing anything if I put my mind to it, as long as I was focused, resilient, and consistent. In his memory and as a way of preserving his legacy, I've spent the last three decades researching, studying, and implementing how ordinary people can have extraordinary levels of mental toughness, so they can achieve what they put their minds to. Thank you, dad, for the gift you instilled in me, and for being the catalyst to help others realize the joy that comes along with achieving their dream. You are missed more than words can express.

Dan, Ryan, and Meg, my kids whom I cherish, admire, and learn from consistently. You are amazing students, athletes, siblings, friends, children, and giving members of your community. I appreciate your love, support, and patience during the process of writing this book. From being my cheerleaders to my sounding boards, this book is inspired by you and is for you. It is also a piece of your grandfather, who is so proud and smiling down on each of you.

Scott, my husband, my advisor, expert creative and marketing director, and never-wavering cheerleader, thank you for your patience, understanding, and support. You stuck with me on the (really) long days, encouraged me when I was discouraged, and celebrated with me every step along the way. This book would not exist without you. Scott, I love you and appreciate you so much.

Pam who is my best friend, confidant, VP of cheerleading, and unapologetically honest sounding board. I can't imagine what the last year, let alone the last thirty years, would have been like without you. Writing a book was hard, and it would have been impossible without experiencing the laughter, tears, setbacks, and celebrations with you.

Mel Abraham, my mentor. I am indebted to you for your wisdom, your integrity, your advice, your time, and of course your invaluable frameworks. It is an honor to be a part of your mastermind to learn and grow my business under your watch. Thank you.

My Think Tank mastermind family, thank you for your wisdom, your accountability, and your advice (that at times was brutally honest).

Brendon Burchard, who showed me the way to high performance and business acumen, and who connected me to some of the most brilliant, compassionate, successful, and joyous souls on the planet.

My High Performance Mastermind family, who are a group of the most selfless, supportive, and impactful people I have ever met. It's a real honor to walk among you and call you my friends and colleagues. Books and successful businesses are not born in solitude, and I am forever grateful for your support. A few of you took extra interest in my mission, showed up for me whenever I asked (and sometimes offered before I had to), and pushed me extra hard. Thank you for making my life temporarily miserable, so I too could achieve what at first seemed impossible.

Ameesha Green, my editor, to whom I am indebted. You understood everything I was trying to accomplish from day one. Your (immense) patience and expertise showed me the way from a basic framework and ideas to a cohesive and impactful book.

Val Sherer, the artist who formatted this book, thank you for your patience, flexibility, and piece of invaluable advice, "It's OK to take a little extra time. Make sure it's right."

Vanessa Moss, my book coach, who showed me the way from an idea to the physical end result of this book and who kept my feet on the ground during the process. I appreciate your guidance and your confidence in me and my message.

To all the research scientists who have proved that "If we did all the things we are capable of, we would literally astound ourselves." – Thomas Edison.

A special mention to K. Anders Ericsson, the author of the acclaimed book *Peak*. I greatly appreciate your wisdom and encouragement. Your research and dedication to the science of expertise is unparalleled. It gives us all hope and proof that we are only limited by what we think is possible and by how deliberately we choose to practice.

FREE COMMUNITY RESOURCES

- Sign up for weekly content and training: www.SherylKline.com

- Worksheets, tools, activities, questionnaires and more: www.SherylKline.com/resources

- Facebook business page: @mentaltoughnesscoach

- Instagram business: @sherylmentaltoughnesscoach

I'm cheering you on and would love to hear from you about any questions, comments, successes, or challenges. Please email me here: Sheryl@SherylKline.com. I read all of my emails personally. Let's do this, together! Here's to you being amazing! 🏆

CONTINUE YOUR TRANSFORMATION

Individuals

- One to one private coaching

- Live Mental Toughness Monthly Round Table

- Your ZONED IN™ DIY coaching program

- Apply: https://www.sherylkline.com/store

- Questions: info@SherylKline.com

Corporate

- Live training, keynotes, and workshops

- Group coaching

- ZONED IN™ Online Training

- Inquire: info@SherylKline.com

REFERENCES

1. Action for Happiness. 2018. *Action for Happiness.* [ON-LINE] Available at: http://www.actionforhappiness.org. [Accessed 9 July 2018].

2. Pychyl, T, 2008. Goal Progress and Happiness. *Psychology Today*, 1, 1-2.

3. Corbin, J, 2017. The Gallup 2017 Employee Engagement Report is Out. *The Gallup 2017 Employee Engagement Report is Out: And the Results... Nothing Has Changed*, [Online]. 1, 1. Available at: https://www.theemployeeapp.com/gallup-2017 [Accessed 4 June 2018].

4. Scottberg, E, 2018. Nine Famous People Who Will Inspire You to Never Give Up. *The Muse*, [Online]. 1, 1-3. Available at: https://www.themuse.com/advice/9-famous-people-who-will-inspire-you-to-never-give-up [Accessed 9 April 2018].

5. CDC. 2006. *about.* [ONLINE] Available at: http://www.cdc.gov/polio/about. [Accessed 7 May 2018].

6. Biography. 2014. *Wilma Rudolph Biography.* [ONLINE] Available at: https://www.biography.com/people/wilma-rudolph-9466552. [Accessed 30 August 2018].

7. Biography. 2014. *Jackie Joyner-Kersee Biography.* [ONLINE] Available at: https://www.biography.com/people/jackie-joyner-kersee-9358710. [Accessed 21 May 2018].

8. Ericsson, Prietla, Cokely, K A, M, E, 2018. The Making of an Expert. *Harvard Business Review*, [Online]. 1, 1-3. Available at: https://hbr.org/2007/07/the-making-of-an-expert [Accessed 9 April 2018].

9. Oxford Reference - Answers with Authority. 2018. *Oxford Reference - Answers with Authority.* [ONLINE] Available at: http://www.oxfordreference.com. [Accessed 30 August 2018].

10. Kelman, H, 1958. Compliance, identification, and internalization: the processes of attitude change. *Journal of Conflict Resolution*, 2(1), 51-60.

11. Gleeson, B, 2016. Why Accountability is necessary for achieving winning results. *Forbes*, 1, 1.

12. Anders Ericsson, K., 2016. *Peak: Secrets from the New Science of Expertise.* 1st ed. New York, New York: Houghton Mifflin Harcourt Publishing Company.

13. Rubin, G, 2009. Stop Expecting to Change Your Habit in 21 Days. *Psychology Today*, [Online]. 1, 1-2. Available at: https://www.psychologytoday.com/us/blog/the-happiness-project/200910/stop-expecting-change-your-habit-in-21-days [Accessed 12 March 2018].

14. Women Making Big Sales. (2017). *The Science Behind Confidence and Motivation.* [Online Video]. 16 May 2017. Available from: https://www.youtube.com/watch?v=o_5jiS-pOp58. [Accessed: 11 September 2017].

15. Dubois, L, 2014. Kimberly Bryant, BE'89, Is Changing the Face of High-Tech with Black Girls Code. *Vanderbilt Magazine*, [Online]. 1, 1-3. Available at: https://news.vanderbilt.edu/vanderbiltmagazine/kimberly-bryant-is-changing-the-face-of-high-tech-with-black-girls-code/ [Accessed 12 March 2018].

16. Main, D, 2014. 2 Percent of People Can Multitask Well. Are You a SuperTasker?. *Popular Science*, [Online]. 1, 1-3. Available at: https://www.popsci.com/article/science/2-percent-people-can-multitask-well-are-you-supertasker [Accessed 15 January 2018].

17. Henriques, G, 2015. How To Foster More Adaptive Thinking. *Psychology Today*, [Online]. 1, 1. Available at: https://www.psychologytoday.com/us/blog/theory-knowledge/201505/how-foster-more-adaptive-thinking [Accessed 15 February 2018].

18. Rampton, J, 2017. Neuroscience Tells Us How to Hack Our Brains For Success. *Entrepreneur*, [Online]. 1, 1. Available at: https://www.psychologytoday.com/us/blog/theory-knowledge/201505/how-foster-more-adaptive-thinking [Accessed 15 February 2018].

19. Adams, AJ, 2009. Seeing is Believing. *Psychology Today*, [Online]. 1, 1. Available at: https://www.psychologytoday.com/us/blog/flourish/200912/seeing-is-believing-the-power-visualization[Accessed 14 March 2018].

20. Taylor, J, 2010. Sports: The Power of Emotions. *Psychology Today*, [Online]. 1, 1-2. Available at: https://www.psychologytoday.com/us/blog/the-power-prime/201012/sports-the-power-emotions [Accessed 13 November 2017].

21. McWilliams, J, 2013. John McEnroe and the Sadness of Greatness. *Pacific Standard*, [Online]. 1, 1. Available at: https://psmag.com/social-justice/john-mcenroe-sadness-greatness-66758 [Accessed 9 April 2018].

22. YouTube. (2010). *Overcoming the Reptilian Brain*. [Online Video]. 12 October 2010. Available from: https://www.youtube.com/watch?v=JQurEc7HRt0. [Accessed: 8 April 2018].

23. Weinberg, R, 2013. Goal Setting in Sport and Exercise: research and practical applications. *Scielo*, 24, 1.

24. Sweeney, M, 2017. Not What We Say or What We Do, but How We Make Others Feel. *Huffington Post*, [Online]. 1, 1. Available at: https://www.huffingtonpost.com/entry/not-what-we-say-or-do-but-how-we-make-others-feel_us_591a2793e4b0f31b03fb9e52 [Accessed 14 May 2018].

25. Seligman, M., 1990. *Learned Optimism*. 1st ed. New York, New York: Alfred A. Knopf.

26 .Starecheski, L, 2014. Why Saying is Believing-The Science of Self-Talk. *NPR*, [Online]. 1, 1-2. Available at: https://www.npr.org/sections/health-shots/2014/10/07/353292408/why-saying-is-believing-the-science-of-self-talk [Accessed 12 March 2018].

27. Campbell, P, 2011. Positive Self-Talk Can Help You Win the Race-Or The Day. *Psychology Today*, [Online]. 1, 1-2. Available at: https://www.psychologytoday.com/us/blog/imperfect-spirituality/201106/positive-self-talk-can-help-you-win-the-race-or-the-day [Accessed 30 January 2018].

28. Lickerman M.D., A, 2010. The Importance of Tone. *Psychology Today*, [Online]. 1, 1-2. Available at: https://www.psychologytoday.com/us/blog/happiness-in-world/201008/the-importance-tone [Accessed 20 February 2018].

29. Carver, M, 2017. 7 Benefits of a Daily Affirmation Plan. *Chopra.com*, [Online]. 1, 1-2. Available at: https://chopra.com/articles/7-benefits-of-a-daily-affirmation-plan [Accessed 20 February 2018].

30. Campbell, P, 2011. Positive Self-Talk Can Help You Win the Race-Or The Day. *Psychology Today*, [Online]. 1, 1-2. Available at: https://www.psychologytoday.com/us/blog/imperfect-spirituality/201106/positive-self-talk-can-help-you-win-the-race-or-the-day [Accessed 30 January 2018].

31. van Schneider, T, 2017. If you want it, you might get it. The Reticular Activating System Explained. *Medium*, [Online]. 1, 1-2. Available at: https://medium.com/desk-of-van-schneider/if-you-want-it-you-might-get-it-the-reticular-activating-system-explained-761b6ac14e53 [Accessed 5 February 2018].

32. Falk PhD, O'Donnell PhD, E, M, 2015. Study Reveals the Neural Mechanisms of Self-Affirmations. *Annenberg School of Communication*, 1, 1.

33. Lynne McTaggart. 2018. *Home.* [ONLINE] Available at: https://lynnemctaggart.com/the-experiments. [Accessed 12 March 2018].

34 Maese, R, 2016. For Olympians, seeing (in their minds) is believing (it can happen). *Washington Post*, [Online]. 1, 1. Available at: https://www.washingtonpost.com/sports/olympics/for-olympians-seeing-in-their-minds-is-believing-it-can-happen/2016/07/28/6966709c-532e-11e6-bbf5-957ad17b4385_story.html?utm_term=.9767d4165d55 [Accessed 9 April 2018].

35. Team USA. 2018. *Home.* [ONLINE] Available at: https://www.teamusa.org/usa-judo/athletes/kayla-harrison. [Accessed 10 April 2018].

36. Munroe-Chandler, K Guerro, M, 2017. Psychological Imagery in Sport Performance. *Oxford Research Encyclopedia*, [Online]. 1, 1-4. Available at: http://psychology.oxfordre.com/view/10.1093/acrefore/9780190236557.001.0001/acrefore-9780190236557-e-228 [Accessed 12 April 2018].

37. Wilson, L, 2017. Top 5 Reasons to Visualize: #3 Improve Skill. *Positive Performance*, [Online]. 1, 1. Available at: https://www.positiveperformancetraining.com/blog/top-5-reasons-to-visualize-3-improves-skill [Accessed 23 March 2018].

38. Mosher, C, 2014. How to Grow Stronger Without Lifting Weights. *Scientific American*, [Online]. 1, 1. Available at: https://www.scientificamerican.com/article/how-to-grow-stronger-without-lifting-weights /[Accessed 26 March 2018].

39. Porter, J, 2014. Do These 3 Things Before Bed to Hack Creativity While You Sleep. *Fast Company*, [Online]. 1, 1. Available at: https://www.fastcompany.com/3031227/do-these-3-things-before-bed-to-hack-your-creativity-while-you-sleep [Accessed 27 March 2018].

40. Adams, AJ, 2009. Seeing is Believing: The Power of Visualization. *Psychology Today*, [Online]. 1, 1. Available at: https://www.psychologytoday.com/us/blog/flourish/200912/seeing-is-believing-the-power-visualization [Accessed 27 February 2018].

41. Popova, M, 2016. The Science of "Chunking," Working Memory, and How Pattern Recognition Fuels Creativity. *Brain Pickings*, [Online]. 1, 1. Available at: https://www.brainpickings.org/2012/09/04/the-ravenous-brain-daniel-bor/ [Accessed 27 February 2018].

42. The Peak Performance Center. 2017. *Chunking Strategy*. [ONLINE] Available at: http://www.ThePeakPerformance-Center.com. [Accessed 16 April 2018].

43. Taylor PhD, J, 2012. Sport Imagery: Athlete's Most Valuable Tool. *Psychology Today*, [Online]. 1, 1. Available at: https://bigthink.com/laurie-vazquez/why-monotasking-needs-to-be-the-new-multitasking-according-to-science [Accessed 26 February 2018].

44. Barraclough, J, 2017. The Importance of Imagery in Sport. *Believe Perform*, [Online]. 1, 1. Available at: https://believeperform.com/performance/the-importance-of-imagery-in-sport/ [Accessed 5 March 2018].

45. Taylor PhD, J, 2012. Sport Imagery: Athlete's Most Valuable Tool. *Psychology Today*, [Online]. 1, 1. Available at: https://bigthink.com/laurie-vazquez/why-monotasking-needs-to-be-the-new-multitasking-according-to-science [Accessed 26 February 2018].

46. But They Did Not Give Up. 2016. *Home*. [ONLINE] Available at: https://www.uky.edu/~eushe2/Pajares/OnFailingG.html. [Accessed 7 May 2018].

47. Sinrich, J, 2017. 19 Successful Women Get Real About The Times They Failed. *Women's Health*, [Online]. 1, 1. Available at: https://www.womenshealthmag.com/life/a19945222/how-to-be-successful-after-failure/ [Accessed 12 March 2018].

48. Sinrich, J, 2017. 19 Successful Women Get Real About The Times They Failed. *Women's Health*, [Online]. 1, 1. Available at: https://www.womenshealthmag.com/life/ a19945222/how-to-be-successful-after-failure/ [Accessed 12 March 2018].

49. Anders Ericsson, K., 2016. *Peak: Secrets from the New Science of Expertise*. 1st ed. New York, New York: Houghton Mifflin Harcourt Publishing Company.

50 Seligman, M., 1990. *Learned Optimism*. 1st ed. New York, New York: Alfred A. Knopf.

51. Chase, C, 2018. 16 Biggest Meltdowns in Tennis History. *USA Today*, [Online]. 1, 1. Available at: https://ftw. usatoday.com/2018/05/tennis-meltdown-karolina-pliskova-andy-roddick-serena-williams-john-mcenroe [Accessed 14 March 2018].

52. Taylor, J, 2010. Sports: The Power of Emotion. *Psychology Today*, [Online]. 1, 1. Available at: https://www.psychologytoday.com/us/blog/the-power-prime/201012/sports-the-power-emotions [Accessed 26 March 2018].

53. Weindling, M, 2017. The Science of Intention. *Uplift*, [Online]. 1, 1. Available at: https://upliftconnect.com/the-science-of-intention [Accessed 13 March 2018].

54. Grant Halvorson, H, 2010. Yes, You Can Stop Thinking About It. *Psychology Today*, [Online]. 1, 1. Available at: https://www.psychologytoday.com/us/blog/the-science-success/201004/yes-you-can-stop-thinking-about-it [Accessed 14 March 2018].

55. Barry Kaufman, S, 2011. Confidence Matters Just As Much As Ability. *Psychology Today*, [Online]. 1, 1. Available at: https://www.psychologytoday.com/us/blog/beautiful-minds/201112/confidence-matters-just-much-ability [Accessed 26 March 2018].

56. Amabile and Kramer, T and S J, 2011. The Power of Small Wins. *Harvard Business Review*, [Online]. 1, 1. Available at: https://hbr.org/2011/05/the-power-of-small-wins [Accessed 30 March 2018].

57. Pattison, K, 2008. Worker, Interrupted: The Cost of Task Switching. *Fast Company*, [Online]. 1, 1. Available at: https://www.fastcompany.com/944128/worker-interrupted-cost-task-switching [Accessed 2 April 2018].

58. Cardiff, S, 2013. Emotions, Memory and Confidence. *Mental Training Inc. blog*, [Online]. 1, 1. Available at: https://mentaltraininginc.com/blog/emotions-memory-and-confidence [Accessed 26 February 2018].

59. Starecheski, L, 2014. Why Saying Is Believing-The Science of Self-Talk. *NPR*, [Online]. 1, 1. Available at: https://www.npr.org/sections/health-shots/2014/10/07/353292408/why-saying-is-believing-the-science-of-self-talk [Accessed 26 February 2018].

60. A+E Networks. 2009. *History.com*. [ONLINE] Available at: https://www.history.com/this-day-in-history/roger-bannister-breaks-four-minutes-mile. [Accessed 2 April 2018].

CPSIA information can be obtained
at www.ICGtesting.com
Printed in the USA
BVHW040452050820
585512BV00008B/15/J

9 781614 310730